The Change²⁰

Insights into Self-Empowerment

Jim Britt ~ Jim Lutes

With

Co-authors From Around the World

The Change[20]

Jim Britt ~ Jim Lutes

All Rights Reserved

Copyright 2024

The Change

10556 Combie Road, Suite 6205

Auburn, CA 95602

The use of any part of this publication, whether reproduced, stored in any retrieval system or transmitted in any forms or by any means, electronic or otherwise, without the prior written consent of the publisher, is an infringement of copyright law.

Jim Lutes ~ Jim Britt

The Change Volume 20

SKU# 2370000270242

Co-authors

Jim Britt

Jim Lutes

Dr. Allison Snowden

Steve Kopshaw

Victor Hailey

Tra Urban

Stacie Shifflett

Shelly Snitko

Shantae Bridges

Samantha Duffy

Rachel Best

Nicole Harvick

Kathryn Brown

Sir James Gray Robinson, Esq.

Gregory Mester, Jr

Fanny Newport

Erin Birch

David Norris

Carla Hooker

Angeline Mitchell

Ana Smith

Amanda Irtz

Alan A. Mikolaj

DEDICATION

To all those who dedicate their life to helping others live a more fulfilled life

PREFACE

Jim Britt

One of the World's top 20 life and success strategists and top 50 most influential keynote speakers

The only constant in life is change. It swirls around us, weaving through the fabric of our existence, shaping our perspectives, molding our characters, and pushing us toward personal growth. Yet, despite its inevitability, change often comes with a veil of uncertainty and fear. How do we navigate these turbulent waters of transformation? How do we harness its power not only to survive, but to thrive?

"The Change-Insights into self-empowerment" is a collective journey into the heart of transformation, a treasury of wisdom from twenty-two diverse voices, each offering a unique perspective on self-empowerment. This anthology is more than a collection of essays; it is a tapestry of experiences, woven together to inspire, guide, and empower readers on their own paths of change.

As the co-creator and publisher of this anthology series, my journey began with a simple question: What does it truly mean to empower oneself in the face of change? The answers unfolded through the secrets and strategies shared by our esteemed coauthors. The depth of their insights reflects the rich tapestry of human experience, and their stories serve as both a mirror and a roadmap for those seeking self-empowerment.

The twenty-two chapters in this book are a testament to the resilience of the human spirit. Each coauthor generously shares their personal journey of transformation, offering glimpses into the moments of struggle, self-discovery and triumph. These writings are as diverse as the coauthors themselves, spanning over thirty countries, cultures, and life experiences. Yet, in their diversity, a common thread emerges—a shared commitment to embracing as a catalyst for personal empowerment.

Within these pages you'll discover several facets of the self-empowerment journey. "Awakening" is where our coauthors explore the pivotal moments that sparked their awareness and sparked their desire for change. Their stories demonstrate the transformative power of self-awareness, the first step on your own path to empowerment.

Next is "Resilience" where you can delve into the challenges our coauthors faced and the strength, they found within to overcome diversity. Whether dealing with loss, facing unexpected detours, or navigating the complexities of personal relationships, or in business, these stories illustrate the transformative nature of resilience and the inherent power within us to adapt and persevere.

Next, you'll find "Empowerment" which is the celebration of the intentional choices made by our coauthors to take charge of their lives. Through conscious decisions, mindset shifts, and a commitment to personal growth, they found the keys to unlocking their true potential. These stories and insights serve as beacons of inspiration for readers seeking to actively shape their own destinies.

And finally, "Integration" as our coauthors reflect on the ongoing journey of self-discovery and personal change. They share their practices, philosophies, and lessons that continue to guide them as they navigate the ever-changing landscape of life. These stories offer a roadmap for readers to integrate and sustain their newfound empowerment into their daily lives.

"The Change" is an invitation to explore the depths of your own potential, to embrace the certainty of change with open arms, and to recognize that within every challenge lies an opportunity for growth. It's a guide for those who seek not to just survive change but to harness its transformative power for a more empowered and fulfilling life overall.

So, as you embark on the journey through the pages of this volume of "The Change" I encourage you to approach each chapter with an open heart and curious mind, realizing that just one good idea acted upon can profoundly change your life. Let the stories and strategies shared by our coauthors be a source of inspiration, guidance, and confirmation that you too possess the power to navigate change with grace and determination and emerge stronger on the other side.

May this anthology serve as beacon of light, illuminating the path of self-empowerment and inspiring you to embrace the infinite possibilities that arise when you courageously and openly welcome change into your life.

With Gratitude and anticipation! Look forward to hearing your success story!

Jim Britt

http://JimBritt.com

FOREWORD

By Les Brown

Many of us spend at least a good part of our day going over internal dialog. We relive past experiences, worry about the future, blame the outside world for our shortcomings and criticize ourselves for not having all we want by this point in our lives. We do this both consciously and unconsciously. Even while we are listening to others, we aren't really fully present. Instead, we are rehearsing our answers, slipping back into yesterday and worrying about tomorrow.

We live in uncertain times. We all feel we have minimum control over being able to change external circumstances, but we do have control over being able to change our internal environment, not only being able to see the truth behind a given situation but also how we respond to it. And to get the best out of the most stressful times, we need to demand the best from ourselves.

Many feel the pain of unhappiness. So many suffer from it daily, unaware that they can eliminate their suffering and find happiness by simply seeing the truth behind their unhappiness and making the right choices to change it. The problem is that our emotional conflicts are so familiar to us that they keep us blinded to better possibilities. We actually become addicted to feeling the way we do, thinking that it is just the way things are and we resign ourselves to getting by and coping.

I have had the privilege of speaking for over forty years serving millions of people from over 51 different countries. I know that there are certain patterns that create success and other patterns that breed internal conflict and failures.

The secret to being fulfilled and living the life you want is having the courage to go beyond the skills you've learned and discover the gifts that you were born with and to implement them daily. So many people settle for less in life, but I can tell you from my experience that it doesn't have to be that way.

I was born in an abandoned building on a floor with my twin brother in a poor section in Miami Florida called Liberty City. When we were six weeks of age, we were adopted by Mrs. Mimi Brown. Whenever I speak, I always say that all that I am and all I ever hope to be I owe to my mother.

When I was in the fifth grade, I was labeled educable mentally retarded and put back from the fifth grade to the fourth grade and failed again when I was in the eighth grade. Mrs. Mimi Brown took my brother and I and five other kids in as foster kids and eventually adopted us.

Because of the work that Jim Britt does and the methods and techniques he uses to change your story and how you see yourself, it enabled me to build my career to make it against all odds. Both Jim Britt and Jim Lutes are icons in personal development and empowering others to be the best they can be.

You have something special inside. You have greatness in you. When you read this book it will take you on a journey and introduce you to a part of yourself that has remained hidden and you didn't know existed.

When you begin to look at your goals and dreams realize that you have greatness inside you. "The Change" will provide the insights and processes of self-development that will empower you to manifest your greatness.

Jim Britt and I actually started the foundation of our speaking careers in the same direct selling company, Bestline, over 40 years ago. Although I haven't followed Jim Britt's career over the years, I do know that he is recognized as one of the top thought leaders in the world, helping millions of people create prosperous lives, rewarding relationships and spiritual awareness. He has authored 15 books and multiple programs showing people how to understand their hidden abilities to do more, become more and enjoy more in every area of life.

Today, Jim Britt and mind programming expert, Jim Lutes, along with inspiring co-authors from around the world, bring a pioneering work "The Change" book series to the market to transform lives. Their principles are forged on touching millions on every continent.

As you read, you are exploring self-empowerment principles from a whole different perspective. In fact, Jim and Jim's publications of The Change book series now has hundreds of coauthors in 26 countries. The real power in each book is that 20 coauthors share their inspiring story so that the reader may benefit from their experience. It is packed with life-changing ideas, stories, tips, strategies on various empowering topics that you will love.

The principles, concepts and ideas within this book are sometimes simple, but can be profound to a person who is ready for that perfect message at the right time and is willing to take action to change. Maybe for one it's a chapter on relationships or leadership. For the next maybe it's a chapter on forgiveness or health awareness, and for another a simple life-changing message like I received as a youngster from a teacher. Each chapter is like opening a surprise empowering gift.

As I travel the world presenting my seminars, I meet people who spend more time and energy focused on what's wrong with society and their lives than is spent on helping each other improve the quality of life. With so much time spent on social media we often fear intimate contact with each other. Mistrust is often our first reaction. We judge and sometimes brutalize those among us who are in any way different from ourselves. We become addicted to anything that allows us a brief consolidation from the terrible pain we feel inside.

We need to begin to understand more about ourselves and our condition if there is ever to be the possibility of a healthy society. I believe this is possible and that's why I am so passionate about the work I do. Simply put…we are at war with ourselves. Real healing only takes place when we are willing to experience and face the truth within.

The conclusion to me is an exciting one. You, me and every other human being are shaping our brains and bodies by the thoughts we think, the emotions we feel, the intentions we hold, and the actions we take daily. Why is it exciting? Because we are in control of all these things and we can change as long as we have the intention, willingness and commitment to look inside, take charge of our lives and make the changes.

Whether you're pursuing, your dreams as an entrepreneur, a business owner or you want a more fulfilling relationship, or simply want to live a happy life, being authentic and actively appreciating what you're really capable of is going to be one of the most important assets you possess. It will make the difference between just "getting by" and really thriving and experiencing happiness or internal conflict.

Self-knowledge provides you with the emotional edge that will help you create a better life not only for yourself, but also for everyone with whom you come in contact.

This is the time to extract the best out of yourself and to use that gift to touch the lives of others.

I want to congratulate Jim Britt and Jim Lutes for making this publication series available and for allowing me to write the foreword. I honor them both and the coauthors within this book and the series for the lives they are changing.

As you enter these pages, do so slowly and with an open mind. Savor the wisdom you discover here, and then with interest and curiosity discover what rings true for you, and then take action toward the life you want.

Be prepared…because your life is about to change.

Hope to meet you one day at one of my seminars. And remember, everything you do counts!

Les Brown

Table of Contents

PREFACE……………………………………...…………..vii

FOREWORD xi

Jim Britt 19
  Think Like Superman

Jim Lutes 31
  What You do with YOU

Steve Kopshaw 51
  The Journey Within: Leading Self to Lead Others

Alan A. Mikolaj 61
  Leading with Meaning & Purpose

Amanda Irtz 73
  Restoring Wholeness: Unearthing the Beautiful Truths in Parenting

Tra Urban 83
  Unlocking Life's Secrets ~ A Journey of Personal Empowerment

Victor Hailey 95
  From Suffering to Hope: A Journey of Personal Development

Kathryn Brown 107
  Hope Road: From Struggles to Surrender, Finding Purpose in Empowering Others.

David Norris 119
  Is it Good to be You?

Erin Birch 127
  A Midlife Crisis or a Midlife Awakening and Transformation

Sir James Gray Robinson, Esq. **135**
  Changing Reality

Angeline Mitchell **145**
  Who is Angeline?

Ana Smith **151**
  Change your Mindset, Change your Life."

Carla Michelle Hooker **165**
  Adversity to Strength: Unveiling Resilience

Rachel Best **175**
  From Dreamer to Achiever. Making a Mark in the World

Nicole Harvick **183**
  Living Beyond the 3rd Dimension

Greg Mester, Jr. **193**
  You Can Thrive in a Lifetime of Change

Stacie Shifflett **203**
  Difficult Women: Awaken Your Extraordinary and Embrace the Power of Transformation

Shantae Bridges **213**
  From Solitude to Triumph - The Entrepreneur's Path of Delegation, Collaboration, and Mentorship 214

Shelly Snitko **223**
  Rising Above the Storm: Embracing Change with Courage

Samantha Duffy **233**
  A Simple Idea

Fanny Newport **239**
  Resilience and Positive Mindset Are Key for Any Business

Afterword **249**

Think Like Superman

The Change[20]

Jim Britt

Jim Britt is an award-winning author of 15 best-selling books and nine #1 International best-sellers. Some of his many titles include Rings of Truth, Do This. Get Rich-For Entrepreneurs, Unleashing Your Authentic Power, The Power of Letting Go, Cracking the Rich Code and The Entrepreneur.

He is an internationally recognized business and life strategist who is highly sought after as a keynote speaker, both online and live, for all audiences.

As an entrepreneur Jim has launched 28 successful business ventures. He has served as a success strategist to over 300 corporations worldwide and was recently named as one of the world's top 50 speakers and top 20 success coaches. He was presented with the "Best of the Best" award out of the top 100 contributors of all time to the Direct Selling industry.

For over four decades Jim has presented seminars throughout the world sharing his success strategies and life enhancing realizations with over 5,000 audiences, totaling almost 2,000,000 people from all walks of life.

Early in his speaking career he was Business partners with the late Jim Rohn for eight years, where Tony Robbins worked under Jim's direction for his first few years in the speaking business.

As a performance strategist, Jim leverages his skills and experience as one of the leading experts in peak performance, entrepreneurship and personal empowerment to produce stellar results. He is pleased to work with small business entrepreneurs, and anyone seeking to remove the blocks that stop their success in any area of their life.

One of Jim's latest programs "Cracking the Rich Code" focuses on the subconscious programs influencing one's relationship with money and their financial success.

www.CrackingTheRichCode.com

Think Like Superman

By Jim Britt

"Waking up to your true greatness in life requires letting go of who you imagine yourself to be."

--- Jim Britt

FACT: Becoming a millionaire is easier than it has ever been.

Many people have the notion that it's an impossible task to become a millionaire. Some say, "It's pure luck." Others say, "You have to be born into a rich family." For others, "You'll have to win the Lotto." And for many they say, "Your parents have to help you out a lot." That's the language of the poor.

A single mother with five children says, "I want to believe in what you're saying. However, I'm 45 years old and work long hours at two dead-end jobs. I barely earn enough to get by. What should I do?"

Another man said, "Well, if you work for the government, you cannot expect to become a millionaire. After all, you're on a fixed salary and there's little time for anything else. By the time you get home, you've got to play with the kids, eat dinner, and fall asleep watching TV."

Everyone has a story as to why they could never become a millionaire. But for every story, excuse really, there are other stories OR PEOPLE with worse circumstances, that have become rich.

The truth is that all of us can become as wealthy as we decide to be, and that's a mindset. None of us is excluded from wealth. If you have the desire to receive money, whatever the amount, you have all of the rights to do so like everyone else. There is no limit to how much you can earn for yourself. The only limitations are what you place on yourself.

Money is like the sun. It does not discriminate. It doesn't say, "I will not give light and warmth to this flower, tree, or person because I don't like them." Like the sun, money is abundantly available to all of us who truly believe that it is for us. No one is excluded.

There are, however, some major differences between rich and poor people. Here are some tips for becoming rich.

Change Your Thinking

You have to see the bigger picture. There are opportunities everywhere! The problem is that most people see just trees, when they should be looking at the entire forest. By doing so you will see that there are opportunities everywhere. The possibilities are endless.

You'll also have to go through plenty of self-discovery before you earn your first million. Knowing the truth about yourself isn't always the easiest task. Sometimes, you'll find that you are your biggest enemy—at least some days.

Learn from Millionaires

Most people are surrounded by what I like to call their "default friends." These friends are acquaintances that we see at the gym, school, work, local happy hour, and other places. We naturally befriend these people because we are all in the same boat financially. However, in most cases, these people aren't millionaires and cannot help you become one either. In fact, if you tell them you are going to become a millionaire, some may even tell you that it's impossible and discourage you from even trying. They'll tell you that you're living in a fantasy world and why you'll never be able to make it happen. Instead, learn from millionaires. Let go of these relationships that pull you down when it comes to your money desires. It's okay to have friends that aren't millionaires. However, only take input from those that have accomplished what you want to accomplish. Hang out with those that will encourage and help you get to the next level. Don't give your raw diamonds to a brick layer to be cut.

Indulge in Wealth

To become wealthy, you must learn about wealth. This means that you'll have to put yourself in situations that you've never been in before.

ON OCCASION, DO SOME OF THESE:

Fly first class and see how it makes you feel.

Eat out at the finest restaurant and don't look at the price.

Take a limo instead of a cab or Uber. Watch how you feel.

Reserve a suite in a first-class hotel.

If you are used to drinking a $20 bottle of wine, go for the $100 and see how it tastes. It does taste different.

All I am saying is, try some of the things that wealthy people do and see how it makes you feel.

Believe it is Possible

If you believe that it is possible to become a millionaire, you can make it happen. However, if you've excluded yourself from this possibility and think and believe that it's for other people, you'll never become a millionaire.

Also, be sure to bless rich people when you can. Haters of money aren't likely to receive any of it either.

Read books that have been written by millionaires. By gaining a well-rounded education about earning large sums of money and staying inspired, you'll be able to learn the wealth secrets of the rich. I just saw a video on LinkedIn with my friend Kevin Harrington from the TV show Shark Tank. He said that one of his new companies just had a million-dollar day on Amazon.

Enlarge Your Service

Your material wealth is the sum of your total contribution to society. Your daily mantra should be, *'How do I deliver more value to more people in less time?'* Then, you'll know that you can always increase your quality and quantity of service. Enlarging your service is also about going the extra mile. When it comes to helping others, you must give it everything you have. You just plant the seeds and nature will take care of the rest.

Seize ALL Opportunities That Make Sense

You cannot say "No" to opportunities and expect to become a millionaire. You must seize every opportunity that has your name on it. It may just be an opportunity to connect with an influential person for no reason. Sometimes the monetary reward will not come immediately, but if you keep planting seeds, eventually you'll grow a fruitful crop. Money is the harvest of the service you provide and sometimes the connections you have. The more seeds you plant, the greater the harvest.

Have an Unstoppable Mindset

Want to know some of what my first mentor shared with me that took me from a broke factory worker, high school dropout, to millionaire?

First, he said, you have to start thinking like a wealthy, unstoppable person. You have to have a wealth mindset. He said that wealthy people think differently. He said, "I want you to start thinking like Superman!" Sounds crazy, right? Well, it's not. It's powerful and here's why. How you think will change your life.

Wealthy people think differently. They really do. And anyone can learn to think like the wealthy.

I'm not talking about positive thinking, Law of Attraction, or motivation. Let's get real. None of that stuff works anyway. Otherwise, we would all be rich and happy already. I'm talking about thinking based in quantum physics science. Once you understand and apply it, it will change your life. You will become unstoppable!

If there was any person, fictional or real, whose qualities you could instantly possess, who would that person be? Think about it. Personally, I would say that Superman is the perfect person. Now, you are probably thinking I have lost it right? Just stick with me here. I think you will like what you are about to hear.

Superman is a fictional superhero widely considered to be one of the most famous and popular action hero and an American cultural icon. I remember watching Superman every Saturday morning when I was a kid. I couldn't get enough. He was my hero!

Let's look at Superman's traits:

Superman is indestructible.

He is a man of steel.

He can stop a locomotive in its tracks.

Bullets bounce off him.

He is faster than a speeding bullet.

No one can bring him down.

He can leap tall buildings in a single bound. Great powers to have in this day-and-age, wouldn't you say? What else would you need?

Now, for all you females, don't worry, we have not left you out. There is also a female version of Superman, named Superwoman. She has the same powers as Superman.

Now, this is where it gets interesting. Let's first look at the qualities that Superman possesses that you want to make your own. And to make it simple, I will refer to Superman for the rest of this message, and you can replace with Superwoman if you are female.

Again:

Superman is powerful and fearless.

Superman is virtually indestructible—except for kryptonite of course.

Superman can stop bullets.

Superman has supernatural powers. He can see through walls.

Superman can stop a speeding locomotive.

Superman can stop a bullet.

Superman jumps into immediate action when troubles arise.

Superman can crash through barriers.

Superman can even change clothes in a phone booth in seconds. Not too many of those around anymore. You'll have to duck behind a building to change.

So, you're thinking right now, *'Ok, I know that Superman has incredible supernatural powers, how can that help me? What good will it do me to think I am Superman, a fictional character?'*

Here is where science comes in. This is the part where you will be amazed when you learn about the supernatural powers that you already possess! NO, REALLY!

Your brain makes certain chemicals called neuro peptides. These are literally the molecules of emotion, like love, fear, joy, passion, and so on. These molecules of emotion are not only contained in your brain they actually circulate throughout your cellular structure. They send out a signal, a frequency much like a radio station sending out a signal. For example, you tune to 92.5 and you get jazz. Tune to 99.6 and you get rock. And if you are just one decimal off, you get static. The difference is that your signal goes both ways. You are a sender and a receiver.

You put out a signal, a mindset, of confidence about your financial success and people, circumstances, and opportunities show up to support your success. When you put out a signal of doubt and uncertainty and you receive support for your doubt and uncertainty. You've been around someone that you didn't trust, or you felt less than positive just being in their presence, right? You have also been around people that inspire you. That's what I'm talking about. You are projecting a frequency, looking to resonate with the frequency you are transmitting.

Anyway, the amazing part about these cells of emotion is that they are intelligent. They are thinking cells. These cells are constantly eavesdropping on the conversation that you are having with yourself. That's right. They are listening to you! And others are listening to your cells as well. Others feel what you feel when they are around you.

Your unconscious mind, your cells, are listening in, waiting to adjust your behavior based on what they hear from you, their master. So just imagine what would happen if you started to think like Superman...or like a millionaire.

Here are some of the thoughts you might have during the day:

"The challenges I face day today are easily overcome, after all I am Superman."

"I am indestructible."

"I have incredible strength."

"Nothing can stop me.....NOTHING."

"I have supernatural powers and can overcome anything."

"I can accomplish anything I want when I put my mind to it."

"I can break through any barrier."

"I can and I will do whatever it takes to accomplish my goal."

"I fear nothing."

The trillions of thinking cells in your body and brain listen, and they create exactly what you tell them to create. Their mission is to complete the picture of the you they see and hear when you talk to them. They must obey. It's their job!

Since you are Superman, you cannot fail. Why? Your thinking cells are now sending out the right signal, because you told them to. They are making you stronger, more successful, everyday! You have the ability to fight off all negativity, doubt, fear, and worry—nothing can stop you!

Superman has total confidence. So, your cells of emotion relating to confidence will now create more neuro peptide chemicals to promote feelings of power and confidence that others will feel in your presence.

Superman is fearless. So, your cells of emotion relating to fear will now create more neuro peptide chemicals to create feelings of courage. You are unstoppable!

And here's the key. Others will respond to you in the same way that you are talking to yourself.

If you are confident, others will have confidence in you.

You have thousands of thoughts every day. Make sure your thoughts are leading you in the direction you want to go. Make sure you are telling your cells a success story, and not a 'woe is me' story.

Most have been conditioned to think that creating wealth is difficult, or that it's only for the lucky few. What do you believe? It doesn't cost you any more to think like Superman; and it's much more inspiring!

Mediocrity cannot be an option if you decide to be wealthy and think like Superman.

Your decision, and communication with your cells, creates a mindset; that mindset influences how you show up.

None of that old type of thinking matters anymore…after all, you are Superman, and you can accomplish anything.

If you want wealth, you have to stretch yourself. You have to do the things that unsuccessful people are not willing to do. You have to say "yes" to opportunity, then figure out how to get the job done.

Maybe you are uncomfortable selling and asking for money. If that's the case, then learn sales and learn to ask for money every day until you feel comfortable asking for it. You will never have money if you don't learn to ask for it.

I've learned a lot in the past 40+ years as an entrepreneur. I've learned that in order to have more, you have to become more. I've also learned that if you are comfortable, you are not growing. I learned that I couldn't go from a nervous rookie speaker with minimal self-confidence to hosting TV shows and speaking in front of 5,000 people overnight. I simply wasn't ready. I grew into that, one speaking engagement at a time. Every time I finished a speaking engagement, I would ask myself, "How did I do, and how could I do it better?" I still do that today.

And I've learned from the hundreds of thousands of people I've trained, coached, and mentored that none of us can do something we don't believe is possible. It's not going to happen if you're not ready to step out of your comfort zone and stretch yourself.

This has led me to understand the single most important principle of wealth-building, that has meant the difference between poverty and riches for people since humans first traded for pelts.

Are you ready?

Come in just a little closer. Listen up!

Every income level requires a different you, a different mindset! If you think that $10,000 a month is a lot of money, then $100,000 a month will be completely out of reach. If you believe that having $5,000 in the bank would make you rich, then $50,000 won't miraculously appear. You will never earn more money than you believe is "a lot" of money.

What you do as a business is only a small part of becoming rich. In fact, there are thousands, if not tens of thousands, of ways to make money—and lots of it. What I've learned over the years is that, by focusing on who you want to become instead of what you need to do, you're going to multiply your chances of getting rich a hundred-fold.

Ask anyone who's found a way to make a large sum of money legally, and he or she will tell you that it's not hard once you crack the code. And cracking the code starts with you and your mindset. The "code" to which I refer isn't a secret rite or ancient scroll. It's not even a secret. It's a certain way of thinking and believing in which you've trained your mind to see money-making ideas.

That's where you see a need in the marketplace, and you jump on the idea quickly. It might involve creating a new product; or, it may just be teaching others a special technique you've learned. It may even require raising capital to start a company or to market a product or idea on social media.

Don't Hold Back. You Have to Take Action to Change.

Start right now to imagine yourself as already having wealth. How would your life be? How would your day unfold? Start to own your wealth mindset now! The subconscious mind is unable to differentiate between actual fact and mere visualization. So, by imagining that you already have it, you're encouraging your subconscious mind to seek the ways and means to transform your imaginary feelings into the real thing.

Find yourself some mentors. Nobody has all the answers. Surround yourself with people that will support, inspire, and provide you with answers that keep you moving in the right direction. If you truly want to attain wealth, have a thriving business, or reach the top of your game in any endeavor, having a qualified mentor is essential.

Okay, lets come in for a landing ...

It is absolutely essential to have a crystal-clear picture of what you want to accomplish before you begin. If you want to attain wealth, you must learn to operate without fear and with a sharply defined mental image of the outcome you want to attain. This comes from thinking like a wealthy person, (like Superman) making decisions like a wealthy person and being fearless (like Superman) when it comes to stepping out of your comfort zone. Look at the end result as something you're already prepared to do, you just haven't done it yet.

Think about this. Your success is something that you have been preventing; it's not something you have to struggle to make happen. The key is to not let fear, doubt, other people, or mind chatter push your success away. You'll find that the solutions taking you toward your goals will come to you in the most unexpected and sudden ways. You don't need the *perfect* plan first. What you need is a perfectly clear decision about your success, the right mindset, the right mentoring, and the ideal way to get you there will materialize.

The greatest transfer of wealth in the history of the human race is happening right now. Are you positioned to get your share?

Remember, in order to get a different result, you must do something different. In order to do something different you must know something different to do. And in order to know something different, you have to first suspect that your present methods need improving.

THEN, YOU HAVE TO BE WILLING TO DO SOMETHING ABOUT IT.

***

For more information on Jim's work:

www.JimBritt.com

http://JimBrittCoaching.com

www.facebook.com/jimbrittonline

www.linkedin.com/in/jim-britt

For free audio series www.RichCode1.com and www.RichCode2.com

http://becomeAcoauthor.com

To find out how to crack the rich code and change your subconscious programming regarding your relationship with money: www.CrackingTheRichCode.com

Jim Lutes

Say the name Jim Lutes and chances are a top performer in your company has attended one or more of his dynamic trainings over the last few years.

Having taught his branded form of human performance since the early 1990s, Mr. Lutes has accelerated top level entrepreneurs throughout his career by conducting training on personal growth and subconscious programming into worldwide markets.

During this time Jim took his skills regarding the human mind, and combining it with training on influence, persuasion and communication strategies he launched Lutes International in the early 1990s. Based in San Diego California Jim has taught seminars for, corporations, sales forces, individuals and athletes. Having appeared on television, radio and worldwide stages, Jim's style, knowledge and effectiveness provide profound results.

"Jim Lutes possesses a unique ability to create performance change in an individual in a fraction of the time it takes his competitors". The core of human's decisions is based on the programs we acquire, reinforce and grow. Combining Jims various trainings individuals can reach new levels of achievement and fulfillment in all areas of life. The results are at times nothing short of astonishing.

"My goal is to take that embryonic greatness that exists inside every person in America, foster it, empower it and then hand them personal strategies based on solid principles that allow them to take that new attitude and apply it to creating a life masterpiece".

What You do with YOU

By Jim Lutes

Most people think that if they can just learn enough, earn enough, get smart enough, then they will BE enough. And they think that when that happens, they can finally relax and be happy. But what happens is that they get so caught up in what they are constantly *doing* that are not focused on how they are *being.*

In other words, they are not focused on their emotional state. When you engage your emotions your subconscious mind begins to get the messages and begins to establish new rules and new behaviors. Then it becomes a way of life and enters your heart and really begins to come from your heart. When it is in your heart then it is truly part of you. When you are really getting it at the deepest level, is when you can begin to anticipate what I am going to say, you know you understand it at a much deeper level right now.

I began to study human performance as a way to make some changes in my own life and when I began to see some serious results, I got so excited about it that I wanted to share it with other people. So I committed my life to learning and sharing what works with others. So, I am a committed lifetime learner and therefore I have been fortunate enough to have had the ability to look at and study just about every approach there is to personal development and success that is available in today's market. I am a strong advocate of clear, simple, workable approaches that get dependable and lasting results.

Because of the vast wealth of information my Life Masterpiece teaching gives you and the amazing results you will get, you will likely find yourself returning to it again and again throughout your life.

No matter how successful we are, or how successful we become, we all need a coach to encourage us, to challenge us, to remind us to live up to our potential. I am going to be here to do that for you each day, and it is both my honor and my privilege to serve you in that way.

Let's get started now.

The person that you are, and that person that you must become in order to put the colors of your life masterpiece where you want them and blend them in just the right combination to create your own unique experience might right now seem like two very different people, but they are one in the same. You are that person right now. I am going to help you uncover your true identity and purpose so that you can then activate the universal laws and make them work for you.

When we let go of all the stories, we have been telling ourselves about who we think we are supposed to be and what we think we are supposed to do and have, we not only free ourselves we free our families, our children, our intimate partners, and our friends in the process. There is no way you can make a difference in yourself without touching somebody else even if it is not your intention.

The Life Masterpiece focus is about what you can do with YOU. If you want to change any circumstance, any relationship, then you must begin with yourself no matter how convinced you are that somebody else or something else must change. Changing yourself can change even the most rigid system and stubborn person. And ANY progress moves you forward. And any movement forward on your part creates the opportunity for every other part of your life to be moved forward as well.

One of the most effective ways for you to reprogram your mind is through what I like to call vicarious experiences. These are the experiences other people have had and I will bring you through their experiences by sharing their stories with you. These stories are not in this book simply to fill it up and make it fat like you find in some books. These stories are the heart and soul of the book because this is how you will begin to reprogram your subconscious and take the information into your heart where it will transform you.

The reason why vicarious experiences are so powerful is because they relate to you and so when you are reading these stories your conscious mind will get go and your unconscious mind will get the lesson.

And when you read some of these remarkable stories and meet some of these people who have gone through some amazing personal transformations, you will begin to realize that no matter who you are, no matter what part of the world you are from or what culture you grew up in, whether you grow up poor, wealthy or somewhere in between, whether you grow up with religion or Monday Night Football, you will begin to realize that we all have the same problems.

So what will happen is you will begin to connect with these people because they have the same problems you have- the same challenges. They are universal. You will then see what the reason is for this is that we all have the same basic needs, our lives are about meeting these needs and that they impact and determine every single thing we do and every decision we make.

Every single habit, behavior, rule or pattern is your unconscious way of trying to get your needs met. And your needs are the same exact needs every other human being on the planet has. We all use different behaviors to get these needs met but they are still the same.

Some of the behaviors we use are positive and healthy and some of them are not quite so resourceful. And this is one of the reasons why even though we all have the same needs and the same problems, we all get different results. We are hard wired with the same needs, but not with the same subconscious programming. And the reason why we all get different results boils down to one thing- standards.

You know, so often in life, we find ourselves in a position where we live life a certain way. We act a certain way. We were raised in a certain way. And through our lives in an effort to avoid pain and still meet our needs, we made critical decisions about who we are and how we think we need to be. And so we believe we know who we are.

But the way we have behaved for years is simply an *adaptation*. Something that happened in response to the desire we had to meet our basic needs- to get the love, or respect, or acceptance from a parent, lover, loved one or peers- caused us to make a key decision and adapt to the circumstances around us. We do not ever realize that for years we have been living something that we are really good at but which is not necessarily our true nature.

One of the things you will learn here is that a single decision has the power to change everything in a heartbeat. In fact, when you stay with me through this you are going to learn about a decision, I made perhaps some time ago that determines the choices you have made in the course of your life up until now. Today he made a decision to pick up this book and begin this journey with me and if you will indulge me for just a few hours the decision to pick up this book might be the decision that changes everything in your life from today on.

Now that you've made the decision to read it, I will tell you what this book can really do for you. It will get you to uncover and maybe for the first time really identify how the role models of your life have affected your subconscious decision-making in ways you never dreamed possible.

Without getting into the actual science behind it, a child's brain works much differently than an adult brain. As you might already know our brains operate using four different wavelengths -- alpha, beta, theta and delta. Most of the time, the adult brain operates at the beta level when we are awake. The beta level is when our eyes are focused in our conscious mind is in control, and we are logical. The alpha level is a level that we must pass through to go to sleep and to wake up, and it's also the most common level is one we are in a trance. Theta is for a deeper trance or dreaming, and delta is for deep sleep.

This means that when we are at the alpha level, we are highly impressionable, because the messages are going directly into our subconscious minds. A child's mind is different because it operates primarily at the alpha level, which is why children are so impressionable. This also means that our parents and other significant people in our childhood had a tremendous impact on the messages that are subconscious mind received and events from our childhood had a strong impact on our self-image, our identity and how we develop as adults. This is why when we speak about reprogramming the subconscious mind is very important to talk about her childhood and her relationship with her parents. This is not done to point fingers or place blame, but to help us understand some of the reasons for the choices that we make for the patterns that we keep repeating and how they carry over from generation to generation.

Even if you feel like you held your own when you were growing up, and that the relationships that you had as a child -- especially the relationship she had with your mother and father -- were strong, and you feel like you are strong as a result. There are still patterns that your subconscious mind is running that no longer serve you. Because it's the tension, the experience of having to deal with all of the events of your past and even the events that happened before you were born in your parent's past -- all of these experiences affect your decision making, your relationships, your finances, your choices, behaviors and life circumstances, even today.

Even if your childhood was perfect and you feel like you honor, respect and love your parents and adore all of your siblings and even if your parents or your greatest role models, you are still affected on many levels and in many ways. And because you decided to read this book, I believe you have some things you would like to change. If you change anything, first you must learn to reprogram your subconscious mind and part of doing so is to understand that the key decisions you made in the past still impact you today.

Our childhood role models deeply affect both our conscious and subconscious decision-making and behavior patterns. We are all examples, and some of us are warnings. We all, at one time or another impact other people. This is one of the reasons why I stress that it is so important to live consciously and be an example.

When I ask people about their belief systems and the habits and patterns that basically control their lives, I am often struck by how few of these beliefs and habits were ever chosen by that person on a conscious level. In other words, the rules that are guiding your life about how to BE in your own life very often picked up unconsciously.

It is incredible how common it is that people start this process, and when they begin to reassess their lives and their relationships with themselves and others in the success they are having or perhaps not having, they discover that much of what has been screwing up their lives, their achievements, their finances, their careers, their intimate relationships, and even their bodies (and I am not talking about the excuse many of us use about genetics. Being the reason, our bodies look the way they do) was influenced by their PARENTS. Not by their parents' problems necessarily, but by somehow trying to be liked, loved or appreciated by one parent. Many times, these decisions also have to do with trying to avoid pain that was inflicted by a parent or other significant role model, or simply standing up to a parent.

We can be 40, 50 or even 80 years old, and we are still living the strategies of a child.

And what's even worse, is it very often when we were a kid, we said, "I'll never be like that!" And here you are today, exactly like that! You don't want to admit it but if you held up a mirror and watched a film of your interactions you would say, "Oh my God, I never wanted to be like that parent." And yet you are. Or perhaps you have done the opposite. Perhaps you have thrown the pendulum the other way and you're not like that parent at all. Now, you are something worse. Or, let's just say you are something else. You are the opposite of the extreme you didn't like. And so now you are another extreme, that doesn't work either. Because no one teaches us this stuff, and so it becomes unconscious. We don't even see it. It's part of the invisible fabric of our thinking and our decision-making every single day.

This book will give you a unique opportunity to look deep inside yourself. It will allow you to look inside of your relationships, your decisions about money, and your decisions about your career, your relationship with God or your higher power, and even your body. It will allow you to understand how your own up bringing us may be influenced you and you probably know a lot of the ways it has influenced you, but maybe you'll spot some of the decisions you have made, maybe even one core decision that has affected your identity.

So, what the heck does identity mean anyway? It can be such a big and often loaded word. Well, I believe identity is the strongest force in the human personality. If you want to know what shapes you the most it's not your capability. It's your identity and the rules you have for who you think you are.

And you know what the challenge is? Most of us defined ourselves a long time ago. And when we step outside that definition, we get uncomfortable, because the strongest force in the human personality is the need to remain consistent with how we define ourselves. Later, we will talk about the human needs referred to earlier. One of them is certainty. What this means is that if certainty is one of the deepest needs we have, then if you don't know who you are, you do not know how to act.

Very early in life, we begin to define who we are. We use labels such as loner, aggressive conservative, sexy, successful, loser, rich or poor.

I work for others. I am ugly. I am smart. I am a procrastinator. I am clumsy. I am athletic. I am thin. I am big boned. What happens is these definitions become self-fulfilling prophecies because nobody wants to be disappointed. Nobody wants to live in a place of uncertainty. So, there may be arranging your identity or in your definition of yourself, but it may not be absolute.

The metaphor that you so often hear what we talk about our comfort zone, is that our comfort zone is like a thermostat. We all have our comfort zone, and it is set by our subconscious mind. So, if your subconscious mind has set your thermostat in a particular area of your life, for example how much money you make, that let's say 45°, and if the temperature drops down to 40°, guess what happens? It doesn't meet your identity. In other words, things are not good enough, whether it be mentally and emotionally financially with your weight (which by the way is the primary reason people whose weight tend to gain it back because they lose it before reprogramming their subconscious mind to reset the thermostat) or whatever.

For example, if you drop down to 40° and your finances and 45° is your identity. This means that 45° is what you must have. Or, if you drop down to 70° in your intimacy and 80° is your identity, then this is what you must have. Whatever it is, when you drop below your comfort zone, you will be compelled to drive to make it better automatically. If your body gets out of control, there is a point at which you go, "that's enough!" You are willing to be a little off your identity but not that much. And suddenly you go on the diet suddenly make the change because you feel the pressure that comes with being inconsistent with your own definition of how you think you should be.

But what most of us fail to recognize is that this happens on the other side as well. Your subconscious mind since your mental thermostat at say 45° for your finances or 80° mentally for how close you want to be with your intimate partner, or 70° for how your body should look and feel,

This is not your *goal*. Your goal is something much larger. This is your subconscious comfort zone or your subconscious definition of yourself. For example, you might think of yourself as big boned, but if it suddenly isn't good enough and you really become overweight, then you change to fit your self-image or your definition of yourself in order to get back into that comfort zone. But also, if it gets better than you expected, perhaps, you lose a lot of weight and get really good shape, or perhaps you lead your company in sales for two quarters in a row when you normally come in third or fourth, or perhaps you jump from 70° in your intimacy, and now you have a relationship that is at 90 or even 100°. You have a really hot, passionate relationship with more passion than you ever have before, or you lose three dress sizes instead of one, or you double your income, whatever it is, your subconscious mind starts talking some sense into you. And your brain goes, "Hello, dude what the heck are you doing? You are 70 degree-er, what in heck are you doing way appear at 90? You can't keep that. That's not gonna last. Get back down to 70° before you get hurt or fail or screw it up. You're in over your head. You're not an entrepreneur. You work for other people."

Wherever your subconscious mind has set your comfort zone based on the way you define yourself, you're going to keep adjusting to stay in that comfort zone. So many times, in these types of programs, people challenge you to get out of your comfort zone, which you can't do consciously. You have to go into your subconscious and reset your comfort zone, just like you would the thermostat. And this will keep happening until you reprogram your subconscious mind with a new identity, and the new comfort zone. Before you set out to make any kind of lasting change, you must reset your subconscious comfort zone.

And what do we do when we exceed our comfort zone? Well, what happened is that the drive to make things better stops. And so you stop growing and gradually you drift back until you reach your comfort zone. Or worse, you start to sabotage. The mental air conditioners kick on and bring yourself right back down to where you think you deserve to be based on your subconscious identity.

For example, if the only kind of love you view as a child was abuse, the only kind of life. You knew was living paycheck to paycheck or in debt, or the only kind of lifestyle you ever experienced with sedentary, whatever it is, even though it might be painful. It is what you know. This becomes your comfort zone and therefore provides the certainty that you need. It becomes your self-definition and what you think you deserve. You begin to think -- not consciously, but unconsciously -- this IS love, this is just the body. You inherited, or that wealth is for other kinds of people, or you're not the right kind of person to make certain kinds of social contacts. Of course, this is not your conscious thinking that this is what is going on in your subconscious.

And therein lays the trouble, or perhaps a better way to say it, the shortcomings with many of the programs you may have tried in the past. They pump you up and felt good about it. They motivated you with affirmations and taught you to use visualization. They've even taught you that the universal laws work for everyone. You may have even made some changes, but they did not last. Because when you're taught these things, you know the stuff in your head on a conscious level. But your identity and self-definition is the thermostat of subconscious mind, so before you can make any substantive or lasting change, first you must reprogram your subconscious mind and change who you are at the deepest level. (Green papers).

In other words, you must become the kind of person who has whatever it is that you want. Visualizing it, affirming it, and even living your life by a new set of standards is not going to work long term until this stuff goes from your conscious to your unconscious and finally into your heart. Not only do you have to DO it, and not only do you have to LIVE it, but you also have to BECOME it. And then you will manifest it.

And that is the difference between the stick figure you are drawing now or the paint by numbers life you have been taught to lead and the masterpiece you are now creating. So, for the colors in our masterpiece is to really live consciously, to be an example, then we have to get conscious about what is shaping us and the thing that shapes you most identity.

Someone who is outrageous will behave, say things differently and move differently than someone who believes they are extremely conservative. They will use a different voice, a different way of moving and a different language. Here is my question for you:

When did you come up with this definition?

When did you decide who you are?

When was the last time you updated it?

Maybe it's time to take another look at who you are today. And maybe you don't have to actually give up your identity. Maybe the identity created for yourself is magnificent, but maybe it's time to expand it. Maybe it's time to add to it. Maybe it's time to open up to a new level of freedom and options.

And when you do that there will be a processional effect in all areas of your life, because we are all connected in a cybernetic loop. If I want to change you, I can try to control you, but that will not change anything. Or I can try to change the system, but that will not last or will be futile. Or I can change me into an ID so that everything changes.

For example, if I change the way I treat you, the way I respond to you, my voice my body my feelings and my emotions by respect for you. It will affect the way you feel and the way you respond back. And the same is true with the universe and higher intelligence. Once you change yourself, reprogram your subconscious, become the person you need to become that the things that you want in your life, then you will begin to receive a different response from the universe in a different result in your life. Then begin to experience your life as a masterpiece.

You will learn that what we value controls what we are willing to do or not do -- in our businesses, and our relationships, with our bodies and with our children. Some people get locked in place into a mindset. I call it being committed to your commitment. For example, have you ever been in an argument, and you were so angry that as the argument progressed, you forgot what you were angry about, and it just became about winning? We've all been there and what happens is we get committed to being angry and said that resolving the argument. Or we get committed to being right, instead of uncovering the truth. When this happens, get so wrapped up in our commitment that we can no longer see the forest through the trees. We lose touch with what we really want, because we get stuck in a mindset, and we get committed to our commitments.

(Judy- discovers a decision she made as a child and uses the discovery to transform her life and her children and grandchildren's lives).

Today, you are beginning a process that can truly change the quality of your life forever and can take that paint by numbers life you might be living now and create the masterpiece called your life. So just for a moment now, what I want you to do is imagine that your life is a painting. And imagine that you have died and are looking down at that painting. What did you leave behind? Is your life, a masterpiece that is cherished and hangs prominently as an example for others of what is possible, or is it a paint-by-numbers life that is packed away in someone's basement?

As you begin this process, I asked for only two things from you:

Your heartfelt desire to make real changes.

The commitment to follow through and do this, as simple or as located as it might seem in the moment.

If you can do just those two things, then the things that you used to call dreams will become part of your daily reality.

Why is it that you can have a person who seems to have superior abilities, talents, skills, and education, at the same time, they don't produce the quality of life they want or that you might expect from them? And why is it, on the other hand, you can have someone who seemingly has every disadvantage -- no family support, the wrong social status, no emotional support, no education, and the wrong background -- and yet they go out and produce results, way beyond what anyone could have expected or even imagined?

The difference in our quality of life is not about our capability, background or education. Human beings, *that means you*, are *all capable* of achieving incredible results, and yet sadly only a few seem to get it.

What people WILL do is very different from what people CAN do.

I want to challenge you right now to start using your WILL muscle, instead of your TRY muscle, which is probably overdeveloped anyhow. I challenge you to start exercising your inborn human power, which is your birthright as a member of the human race, your ability to act based on the choice and free will that every human has in equal measure. Frankly, this means that if it has been achieved, then there is no reason on earth why you cannot achieve it. And beyond that, if it can be imagined, then there is also very little reason why you cannot achieve it. As a matter of fact, your unconscious mind will rarely imagine something that you are capable of. That is the difference between desires and fantasies. It's true. There are no excuses anymore. If you are reading this and you are a human being that you have the ability to take action and to produce results.

The disability that I'm talking about is not something I can give you. Why? Because you already have it. You were born, great. Now, I challenge you to go out and take back what is rightfully yours.

Hopefully, something is now a weekend within you in two ways. One, by igniting your desire and two by showing you some simple systematic strategies on how you can get greater results on a daily basis.

When most of us think of success or failure, we tend to think of these monumental things. Failure is not an overnight thing, and neither is success.

Just what is success? Well, some people describe it in terms of achievements like a resume. But it is different for everyone. So, some people describe it as a feeling.

The truth is that success is wrapped up in failure. What I mean by that is that success is simply a string of failures all going in the same purposeful direction. That's right. If you want to find success you have to look inside a failure. In other words, if you want to be more successful than the next person, then you simply have to be willing to experience more failure, but not just any failures. You must be willing to take specific actions, based on specific decisions, that may fail most of the time, but keep going, perhaps with a new strategy, experience and more failures, and eventually you will succeed. If this sounds painful, then I want you to think for a moment about what true failure actually is.

True failure is lifelong failure. It is the failure of inactivity. It's not actually failing at what you DO -- those things will lead to success. But when you fail to DO, you fail to succeed. In failing to do is a recipe for ultimate failure in life. When you fail to make the calls, when you fail to follow through, when you fail to say I love you, when you fail to give your all, that is what creates the ultimate failure in life. Ultimate failure creates the greatest pain, the feelings we want to avoid at all costs. Now *that* is painful.

Success happens one step at a time. Success happens one failure at a time. It is successfully making the calls and doing it no matter how long it takes for the outcome in the moment. It is successfully getting up and following through. It is successfully making sure that you make that unique contact. It is successfully breaking through the limits that used to stop you.

Success is a combination of all those little things -- those little successes that often come disguised as failures -- over each day and over your lifetime that eventually create a life that you will have total pride and great joy in knowing that you created your life and made it into a masterpiece of your very own -- a life that is an example to others as how it is done.

The purpose of Life Masterpiece is to show you how to tap the power you were born with and how to tap into it every single day. And to make it an effortless process so that it becomes a lifestyle.

Before I go any further, I want to thank you for your friendship. Even though I have never met you, personally, I feel as if you and I are kindred spirits. The reason why say that is it you picked up this book. You made an investment. You're now reading it. This means you are one of the few who will do what others will not. This puts you light years ahead of 99% of the people. You and I encounter every day. Those people are living a paint-by-numbers life. They want to change, but they just do not get it, because they haven't got the first clue what they want and worse, they are not willing to do anything to change it.

I know you're special because you are researching and exploring and because you are reading this. It says something to me about you. It tells me that you are willing to do what it takes to succeed. It tells me that you are not satisfied with your life, and you will not be satisfied until you have successfully created your own masterpiece. So, I really want to give you the tools that can make a difference.

I have dedicated my life to understanding what makes people do what they do. What drives you? What is it that makes the difference in performance from one human being to the next? If we are all born with the same stuff, what causes some to tap into it and others to settle for a mediocre, paint-by-numbers existence?

Power comes from concentrating your focus and taking daily action to improve something. Even a 1% improvement today can result in unbelievable change, because 1% per day will not give you a 365% difference in being the year, because it builds and compounds to create a difference, way beyond anything you can probably imagine right now.

I will show you how to make it happen quickly, not 10 or 20 years from now, but today. Anything you commit to and focus on everyday must improve.

The challenge is that most of us do not know WHO we are, and therefore do not know how to control our mental focus. In fact, most of us focus on what is not working and spent most of her energy focusing on what we DON'T want by asking questions like, "how come this always happens to me?" If you focus on that enough, then that is what you will continue to experience. (Universal laws don't work unless you reprogram).

I am going to show you how to refocus your mental energy and reprogram your subconscious, so that you can ask better questions and therefore get a better result. Whatever you focus on, you

The Change[20]

manifest, which is why the Law of attraction won't work until you know what you want at the deepest level of your mind.

The key is to get you to live by those factors. Most people focus on the small stuff. I know you are to believe this, or you would not have picked up this book. Most people are so focused on what they have to DO. In other words, they focus on their to-do list, how to make a living instead of how to create their life. You could so easily get caught up in the day-to-day experiences that you tend to make a monument of the port in your mind, when actually in the long term these things that seem monumentally important now are actually quite trivial.

To create your masterpiece, you have to learn how to take care of the big things -- each color in your crayon box -- mentally, emotionally, physically, financially, and spiritually. Here are two things that usually lead to ultimate success -- either inspiration or desperation. Desperation can be a good thing because until you get really dissatisfied. You won't do anything to take your life to another level. Dissatisfaction is awesome! If you are completely satisfied, you will get comfortable. They may life begins to deteriorate.

My guess is that you invested in this book because on some level you are dissatisfied.

("If you make enough money, at least you can handle your problems in style" R)

(Lots of money, beyond comfort zone)

"It's a funny thing, the more I practice the luckier I get" AP

Subconsciously, most of us have an idea of what we think we deserve. This is our comfort zone, which the subconscious mind determines when it sets our internal thermostat. Your subconscious mind has set your internal thermostat, and so when you begin to achieve, perhaps make a lot of money, you begin to sabotage your success dropping down to where you subconsciously think you deserve to be.

The past does not equal the future. Even if you are jaded and cynical, you've tried everything, this moment is a great new opportunity if you've tried other programs in the past that nothing has really changed your lifelong term. I believe that all it has done is it has prepared you for this program. And at some level if you did not believe that, then you would not be reading this right now.

Life Masterpiece is very different from other programs you may have tried. You will not find affirmations and visualizations and motivations in this book. What you will find is the answer to what is keeping you back, and how to reprogram your subconscious mind and how to use it to create.

Your brain is the most powerful computer on the planet. When you learn to use it properly, you can create any result you want. And they can give you the answer to almost any problem you have. The problem is that this computer, we call our brain, is not user-friendly, and does not come with an owner's manual. Life Masterpiece will show you how to operate your supercomputer with precision. Lasting change is not created in your life by learning more. Lasting change is created by using your own power to take action.

We're going to recondition the way your mind works by reprogramming your subconscious. This will change the way you feel and the way you behave for the rest of your life. Just as there have been extraordinary technological, scientific, and medical breakthroughs in the past two decades there has also been a breakthrough in the science of quantum physics. While we are not going to learn specifically about quantum physics in this book, we are going to take and use part of that technology. Because the latest cutting-edge tools for creating lasting change come from breakthroughs in quantum physics that have to do with human technology and how to get new results in record time.

There are four steps to success:

1. Know what you want. It is important for you to know what you want, and for you to know how you want things to turn out. In other words, you must know your outcome before you begin. The first step is to decide what you want out of whatever situation you are currently in. The clearer you aren't what you want, the more you will empower your brain to give you the answers.

2. You must use it. In other words, you must get yourself to take action toward your outcome. This means that you must put energy in the right direction, even when you do not know exactly what to do. Many people do not know what to do first. I will teach you exactly what to do. Some people want to know what happens if they try, and it doesn't work. I can tell you right now, and you will learn why in this book, why nothing you try will ever work. So how do you take action? Decide to. It's not about what you can do. It's about what you will do.

3. Notice your results. It's not enough to take action. You must also pay attention to the results you are getting from your actions. Do your actions always work? No. Remember, success is just a series of failures, but failures with the purpose, failures directed at a specific result. You know what you want; you took action, now notice the result. (JS-obstacles and timing).

4. Be flexible and willing to change your approach. You must be willing to make changes and adjustments based on the results of your actions, because flexibility is the key to the system. In other words, if you notice that what you are doing is not working. And you're not getting closer to your goal or even getting further away, instead of feeling like a failure in giving up. Sometimes you simply need to change your approach.

There is a way to speed this up. Instead of just knowing what you want, taking random actions, I will show you a way to increase the pace and the certainty of your success.

("Knowledge is not power. Knowledge is potential power." R)

You may be thinking, "Jim, if this is a simple, how come everyone isn't doing it?" The answer is because the majority of people tend to get caught up in the day-to-day trivialities such as paying their bills. Now, paying your bills might seem monumentally important to you, but honestly, can you think of anyone who has ever reported that they were successful in life because they mastered the art of bill paying? I am not saying that you shouldn't pay your bills, what I'm saying is that you should know I yourself to get caught up in something trivial and make it something big, so that you can use it as an excuse for not doing the really important things in life. At the end of your life, no one is going to remember whether or not you paid all of your bills and what a wonderful job you did of it. In other words, people get caught up in making a living instead of creating a life. They come to the end of their life dissatisfied because they realize they only live 10% of it, not because they were not capable or intelligent, and not for a lack of knowledge, but simply because they never had a clear idea about what they wanted.

Some people think that what they really want is a program that deals with only one area of your life like that business program. If that is what you are thinking, let me tell you right now that Life Masterpiece is one of the most powerful business programs because it deals with the source of all your business -- YOU. When you are better will be a better speaker, salesperson negotiator. Your creativity will flow freely. Mobile to manage and influence people far more effectively than you can now. The first step to changing your career and your business is to change yourself.

***

www.lutesinternational.com

info@lutesinternational.com

https://www.facebook.com/jimluteshttps://mindmotionacademy.com

Steve Kopshaw

As a seasoned expert in business operations and leadership, my professional journey is marked by a series of successes in steering multiple companies toward significant growth in both their top and bottom lines. My approach to business is deeply rooted in the philosophy that strong relationships are the backbone of any successful enterprise. This belief has guided my leadership style, making me a staunch advocate for empathetic and effective management. My experience spans various industries, where I've not only enhanced operational efficiencies but also cultivated dynamic teams and work cultures. Recognized for my ability to connect with people at all levels and my keen insight into market trends and organizational dynamics, I've dedicated my career to unlocking the potential of businesses and individuals alike. My leadership ethos revolves around the idea that true leadership is about inspiring and enabling others to achieve their best, creating a ripple effect of success and innovation.

The Journey Within: Leading Self to Lead Others

By Steve Kopshaw

Meet Rocky Roads, a normal guy with high ambitions... but he keeps getting stuck. He starts new endeavors and does not finish them. He struggles to create buy-in at work and often walks away, blaming others. Rocky has started multiple diets, only to land right back where he started, well, maybe a few thousand dollars short because of all the programs and supplements he's bought but hasn't seen results from.

See, Rocky is one of us. He lacks a key element, a key understanding of unlocking true success for himself. Leadership. It's a concept widely known for organizational success and professional development, but it's as important, if not more, when it comes to personal growth and achieving your own goals, both personally and professionally.

Rocky, like most of us, often finds himself at the crossroads of life's myriad challenges. And guess what? Life will always present challenges, but it's your ability to navigate them that is more important than the challenges themselves.

Rocky found himself sitting on the couch again, watching some shows and drinking an extra glass or two of wine. It was his normal end to a long, stressful day, usually after he beat himself up for not eating a balanced dinner and recommitting to go to the gym tomorrow. He watched his shows until after midnight, remembered to set his alarm for 5am but we all know how that turned out... zero chance he was actually going to get up. And so, the vicious cycle continued.

Rocky Roads' typical evening ritual on the couch was more than just a routine; it was a reflection of the larger cycle he found himself trapped in. Each night, as he sat there, the TV flickering in the background, a glass of wine in hand, his mind raced with thoughts of what he could have done differently that day. He was adept at identifying where others fell short, but tonight was different. As the clock ticked past midnight, a moment of uncomfortable clarity washed over him.

He realized that the common denominator in all his unfulfilled endeavors and failed attempts at change was not the circumstances, nor was it the people around him; it was he himself. The recognition was a jolt to his system. For the first time, Rocky faced the uncomfortable truth: his lack of commitment and accountability was holding him back.

This realization was a pivotal moment for Rocky. It was the first step towards authentic leadership, a concept he had often heard about but never truly internalized. Authentic leadership was about being genuine, self-aware, and responsible for one's actions. It was about leading oneself before leading others, and at this moment, Rocky understood that he had been failing in that initial step.

He looked at the unfinished projects, the unmet fitness goals, the strained relationships at work, and saw a pattern of avoidance and blame. But now, instead of deflecting these as external failures, Rocky began to see them as reflections of his own decisions. He recognized that true leadership, the kind that could transform his life, had to start with honesty and accountability towards himself.

As he sat there, contemplating this new perspective, Rocky felt a mix of emotions. There was guilt for not realizing this sooner, but also a burgeoning sense of hope. Acknowledging the problem was the first step in addressing it, but he knew that realization alone was not enough. The path to authentic leadership and self-improvement was long and would require more than just self-awareness; it would require action and change.

Yet, at that moment, Rocky made a promise to himself. He would no longer be the spectator in his life, watching passively as opportunities and dreams slipped away. He would take ownership of his actions and decisions, however daunting that might be. This night, though ending like so many before, marked the beginning of a new chapter in Rocky's life, one where he would start taking the reins and steer towards the change he so desperately sought.

In our exploration of authentic leadership, much like the journey we've seen with Rocky Roads, we discover it's a concept deeply rooted in the principles of self-awareness, integrity, and continuous growth. Authentic leadership begins with self-leadership, where a clear understanding of one's values, beliefs, and emotions is paramount. It's about embodying integrity and authenticity, ensuring one's actions are consistent with their words and true to their core values. This form of leadership is not only about recognizing one's strengths and weaknesses but also about taking responsibility and accountability for one's actions and decisions. It is a commitment to continual personal development, where seeking feedback and embracing learning opportunities are seen as pathways to growth and improvement.

When it comes to leading others, authentic leadership transforms into a practice of building trust through transparency and honesty. It involves creating an environment where empathy and understanding are not just encouraged but actively practiced. This kind of leadership empowers others, allowing team members the autonomy to develop their skills and achieve their goals, while also providing the necessary support and resources. Authentic leaders inspire and motivate those around them by leading through example. They demonstrate commitment, passion, and resilience, igniting a similar drive in their team members.

The interplay between self-leadership and leading others in the realm of authentic leadership is a dynamic and interconnected process. As one cultivates self-awareness and integrity within themselves, it naturally influences and enhances their ability to lead others effectively. Leaders who embark on this path of authentic self-leadership become beacons of inspiration, fostering a culture of trust, respect, and continual learning within their organizations or groups. Thus, authentic leadership, in essence, is a journey of being genuine and self-aware, both in leading oneself and others. It's about creating a lasting impact that resonates on both a personal and professional level, much like the path we've seen Rocky Roads traverse in his quest for self-improvement and leadership.

As Rocky Roads absorbed the principles of authentic leadership, a significant shift began to manifest in his daily interactions, especially at work. One day, this shift became strikingly apparent. It was during a team meeting that Rocky, usually preoccupied with his own thoughts and responses, chose to actively listen to a colleague,

Sarah, who was sharing challenges she faced on a project. For the first time, Rocky truly heard her – not just the words, but the frustration and stress behind them. He asked thoughtful questions, showing genuine interest and concern. The connection that ensued was unlike any he had experienced before; it was deeper, more sincere.

This interaction was a revelation for Rocky. He recognized that empathy was more than a professional skill; it was a bridge to authentic human connection. That evening, as he reflected on his day, he realized that his interaction with Sarah was not just about understanding her perspective; it was a moment of connecting with another person on a profound level. This realization made him think about his own relationships and how, perhaps, he had been skimming the surface when it came to truly understanding and connecting with others, including himself.

Empathy stands at the core of meaningful human connections. It's the ability to genuinely understand and share the feelings of another, to see the world through their eyes and to feel what they feel. This powerful tool goes beyond mere sympathy; it involves a deep emotional engagement that fosters understanding, compassion, and connection. In the workplace, empathy transforms relationships, creating environments where trust and cooperation flourish. Leaders like Rocky, who embrace empathy, not only improve their interactions with team members but also inspire a culture of mutual respect and collaboration.

However, the role of empathy extends beyond our interactions with others; it's equally important in how we relate to ourselves. Self-empathy involves recognizing and accepting our own emotions and experiences with kindness and understanding. It's about giving ourselves the same level of compassion and patience that we would offer to someone else. For Rocky, this meant acknowledging his feelings of frustration or inadequacy without harsh judgment, understanding his own needs and limitations, and using this understanding to grow and evolve.

Rocky's newfound understanding of empathy started to reshape his communication style. At work, he had already seen the benefits of empathetic listening and understanding, but the real test came when he met his old friend, Mike, for coffee. Mike had always been the kind of friend who told it like it was, often without much tact. In the past, Rocky's interactions with Mike were marked by superficial conversations, mostly avoiding any real depth or vulnerability.

This time, however, Rocky approached the conversation differently. Inspired by his recent experiences at work, he decided to be more open and direct, but with a layer of compassion that had been missing before. When Mike casually asked how things were going, Rocky took a deep breath and shared not just the successes but also his struggles and doubts, especially about his recent self-improvement journey.

To Rocky's surprise, Mike responded with an understanding he had never shown before. The conversation took a turn, becoming more meaningful than any they had in years. Rocky realized that his honest and direct approach, tempered with empathy, had opened a door to a more authentic connection. He was learning that compassionate communication wasn't just about being kind; it was about being real, about showing up as one's true self while also considering the other person's feelings and perspectives.

This experience with Mike illuminated another facet of Rocky's journey. He saw how the principles of empathetic leadership and communication applied not just in a professional setting but in all areas of life. By being both compassionate and direct, Rocky was able to break down barriers and deepen his relationships. This approach didn't just enhance communication; it enriched his connections, bringing a newfound depth and authenticity to them.

Rocky Roads' experience with his friend Mike provides a perfect segue into understanding the broader concept of compassionate communication while still being direct, and how such an approach can significantly impact all areas of one's life.

Compassionate communication, coupled with directness, is a powerful tool that balances empathy and honesty. It involves expressing oneself clearly and straightforwardly, without sacrificing kindness and understanding. This method of communication is not just about conveying information; it's about connecting with others on a deeper emotional level. When you communicate compassionately, you validate the other person's feelings and perspectives, creating a safe space for genuine dialogue and mutual understanding.

This approach has profound implications both personally and professionally. In personal relationships, being both compassionate and direct fosters stronger bonds built on trust and respect. It encourages openness and vulnerability, allowing people to share their true thoughts and feelings without fear of judgment or misunderstanding. Such honest exchanges deepen relationships, making them more resilient and fulfilling.

In the workplace, this style of communication can transform team dynamics. It creates an environment where feedback is given and received in a constructive manner, where concerns are addressed effectively, and where every team member feels heard and respected. This not only boosts morale but also increases productivity and collaboration. Leaders who practice compassionate but direct communication, like Rocky, inspire their teams to be more engaged and committed, enhancing the overall performance of the organization.

In essence, the practice of compassionate communication while being direct is about striking a balance between honesty and empathy. It's about being truthful without being hurtful, and understanding without being passive. This approach can revolutionize the way we interact with others, leading to more meaningful connections, enhanced teamwork, and personal growth. Just as Rocky discovered through his interactions, embracing this style of communication can be transformative, paving the way for more authentic and rewarding relationships in every sphere of life.

As we observe Rocky Roads' transformative journey, his development of key skills such as resilience, resourcefulness, and integrity intertwine and illustrate how these attributes are essential for personal and professional growth. These skills are not just beneficial for leaders like Rocky but are vital for anyone seeking to navigate life's challenges effectively and ethically.

Resilience is the ability to withstand and bounce back from adversities. It's about maintaining a positive attitude and a sense of purpose in the face of difficulties. Developing resilience involves a mindset that views challenges as opportunities for growth rather than insurmountable obstacles. This skill is crucial in today's ever-changing world, where adaptability and perseverance are key to overcoming setbacks and moving forward.

Resourcefulness, on the other hand, is about being innovative and creative in solving problems, especially in situations with limited resources. It entails thinking outside the box and finding efficient ways to overcome challenges. Resourceful individuals, like Rocky, are adept at leveraging available resources, finding alternative solutions, and approaching problems from different angles. This skill is particularly valuable in professional settings where strategic thinking and the ability to maximize limited resources can significantly impact success.

Lastly, integrity is the foundation of trust and credibility. It involves being honest, ethical, and consistent in actions and decisions. Integrity is about aligning one's actions with one's values and principles, even when it's challenging. For individuals and leaders alike, maintaining integrity builds trust and respect from others and fosters a culture of transparency and ethical behavior. In both personal and professional realms, integrity is essential for building lasting, meaningful relationships and for establishing oneself as a reliable and honorable individual.

In essence, the development of skills like resilience, resourcefulness, and integrity is fundamental to navigating life's complexities. These skills enable individuals to face challenges with confidence, innovate under pressure, and maintain ethical standards. Just as Rocky discovered, cultivating these qualities enhances not only professional capabilities but also enriches personal character, leading to a more fulfilling and impactful life journey.

As we return to the story of Rocky Roads, we see a man who has not reached the pinnacle of all his ambitions but has made significant progress in his journey. Rocky's story is a vivid illustration of the principle that it's progress, not perfection, that truly matters in personal and professional development.

Rocky, once stuck in a cycle of unfulfilled endeavors and self-blame, now stands at a point where he can appreciate the strides he has made. He hasn't achieved all his goals yet – the unfinished projects at work are progressing, his fitness journey has seen more consistent efforts than drastic results, and his relationships, though improved, are still evolving. But Rocky has learned an invaluable lesson: the importance of acknowledging and celebrating progress, no matter how small.

He now understands that personal and professional growth is not a destination to be reached but a continuous journey. This shift in perspective has brought a sense of peace and fulfillment to Rocky's life. He no longer berates himself for not being perfect or for not having all the answers. Instead, he takes pride in his resilience, his newfound resourcefulness, and the integrity with which he approaches each day.

In his moments of reflection, Rocky acknowledges the work that still lies ahead. He knows that there will always be challenges to overcome, skills to develop, and goals to aspire to. But he's learning to enjoy the journey, to find joy in the little victories and lessons learned along the way. He appreciates the progress he's made in empathetic communication, the stronger connections he's built at work and with friends, and the inner strength he's developed.

As this chapter of Rocky's story concludes, we leave him on a high note, with a sense of optimism and a commitment to continual growth. Rocky's journey reminds us all that the pursuit of personal and professional development is an ongoing process, where each step forward, no matter how small, is a step in the right direction. His story is an encouragement to embrace our own journeys, to measure success not by the absence of imperfections but by the progress we make, and to find joy and fulfillment in the continual pursuit of becoming better versions of ourselves.

As we close this chapter, following Rocky Roads' inspiring journey of growth and self-discovery, we turn now to you, the reader. Rocky's story is more than a narrative; it's a call to action, an invitation to embark on your own journey of self-leadership and personal development.

Challenge yourself to lead at a higher level than ever before. Reflect on your own life, your habits, your decisions, and ask yourself where you can make changes, however small they may seem. Like Rocky, you may find that the greatest hurdles often lie within – in our ingrained habits, our unchallenged norms, and our unexamined beliefs. It's in the confrontation and reshaping of these elements that true growth begins.

Simply imagine a world where when you make a promise to yourself, you know that you are going to follow through.

Encourage yourself to step out of your comfort zone, to question the 'norms' that have dictated your actions and decisions. What aspects of your life could benefit from a fresh perspective, a new approach? Remember, it's not about achieving perfection or an unrealistic ideal. It's about progress, about being a little better today than you were yesterday, and even better tomorrow.

Consider the skills that Rocky embraced – resilience, resourcefulness, integrity, and empathetic communication. How can these be woven into the fabric of your daily life? How can they reshape the way you interact with others and with yourself? The journey towards self-leadership is personal and unique to each individual, but the core principles remain the same: self-awareness, honesty, and a commitment to continual growth and improvement.

As you move forward, take inspiration from Rocky's realization that the journey itself is as important as the destination. Embrace your own path with openness and curiosity. Celebrate your progress, learn from your setbacks, and keep moving forward with determination and resilience.

***

To contact Steve:

kopshaw@gmail.com

Alan A. Mikolaj

Alan A. Mikolaj is on a mission to partner with like-minded leaders who aspire to make a positive difference in the world. With his professional expertise, unwavering positivity, and passion, he serves as a sought-after speaker, expert in leadership and organizational development, change agent, author, and coach. Continuously driven by his quest for knowledge, Alan remains a committed student of psychology, leadership, and personal and professional growth and development. Together with his wife and their twin boys, he resides in coastal southeast Texas near Houston, Texas.

Throughout his career, Alan has provided coaching services to leaders across all levels, from the front lines to the C-suite. As a member of the International Coaching Federation (ICF), he upholds and adheres to the organization's high Standards of Behavior and Code of Ethics.

Alan brings extensive experience in leading teams, designing, and delivering engaging and interactive leadership development programs and curricula, both in-person and virtually. He holds certifications as a facilitator in renowned programs and workshops, including The Leadership Challenge®, Leading at the Speed of Trust®, and Crucial Conversations®. Moreover, Alan possesses substantial expertise in conducting and coaching leaders on 360-degree leadership assessments. He is a passionate champion for leading with meaning and purpose.

Alan holds his Master of Arts degree in Clinical Psychology from Sam Houston State University and has extensive experience teaching in higher education.

Leading with Meaning & Purpose

By Alan A. Mikolaj

It was the mid-1960s, a time when the world was experiencing significant changes. There were only three television stations: ABC, CBS, and NBC. The space race was on, the Civil Rights Movement was at a crucial point, and Beatlemania was taking the world by storm. In the midst of this era, my parents were living what seemed to be the American dream. My father, a second-generation Czech-American, worked as an airline mechanic for Braniff International, while my mother, a first-generation Czech-American, embraced the role of a homemaker. Together, they had overcome hardships, including the Great Depression and World War II, and had managed to achieve middle-class status. Our family lived in a charming 3-bedroom, 2-bathroom house in the southern end of Houston not far from Hobby airport. We owned a car, a truck with a removable camper, and a small fishing boat. To the outside world, my parents had "made it."

As a young child of about four or five years old, I had little awareness of their journey. My days were filled with joy as I immersed myself in watching reruns of *The Adventures of Superman* and *The Lone Ranger* on Saturday mornings, eagerly reenacting the heroic adventures of these characters at every opportunity.

One of my earliest memories, and a lesson that profoundly impacted my life, was when my mother called me over with a serious tone in her voice. She had an important question to ask.

"Alan, what's going to be your vocation?" she inquired.

It was a deep question to pose to such a young child, and she continued to revisit it in various forms until my senior year of high school.

The word "vocation" originates from the Latin word "vocāre," which means 'calling.' In asking about my vocation, my Catholic mother was inquiring about how I would respond to God's call and discover His purpose for my life. While this chapter is not intended to be religious, it resonates with those who hold spiritual beliefs, as they can draw strong connections between the insights I share and their own convictions. The true intent here is to provide context for one of the most profound lessons I've learned about life and leadership—an insight that originated from my mother when I was just a young boy.

As children, we are often asked, "What do you want to be when you grow up?" In reality, people are inquiring about our future professions or job roles, focusing on the external aspects. Rarely are we encouraged to explore who we want to be, the purpose of our existence, and how we will respond to the profound gift of life itself. The former question centers on meeting others' expectations—an outside-in perspective. However, the latter question delves into introspection and self-inquiry—an inside-out approach. Opportunities to engage in this deep introspection, contemplating our life purpose, principles, and values, are scarce for most of us. I was fortunate to have a mother who encouraged this process. Nevertheless, finding clear answers did not come easily. It took over 20 years, extending beyond my childhood, to arrive at a clearly defined and articulated life mission statement. And it took an additional 25 years for that mission statement to evolve into a philosophy of leadership.

This chapter aims to explore the significance of personal meaning and purpose for leaders, regardless of their organizational context or level of influence. Over the past 15 years, I have had the privilege of working with leaders across various roles, from frontline positions to the C-suite. None of these leaders pursued their roles with the aim of being ordinary or maintaining the status quo. They all aspired to make a positive difference in the world. However, achieving exceptional leadership and extraordinary outcomes can often feel elusive.

A Rose by any Other Name

Imagine transforming your career and achieving extraordinary success like the Director of Imaging who went on to write a book and be invited to completely rebuild the radiology department for a hospital system, or the Director of Ambulatory Services who recently secured the position of Vice President of Operations at a renowned healthcare system, or the Director of Business Development who now serves as the esteemed Vice President and COO in a major healthcare organization, or the Chief Nursing Officer who ascended to the role of CEO in a thriving rehabilitation hospital.

What's their secret? They all share a common thread—through their partnership with me, they developed their first leadership philosophy statement. They began leading with greater meaning and purpose.

A leadership philosophy statement can take various names within the realm of personal meaning and purpose. It can be referred to as a life mission, a personal operating system, a calling, playing your own game, having a personal code or set of standards, your voice, your why, or a leadership legacy statement. Warren Buffet calls it his 'inner scorecard'[1] or, in my mother's words, a vocation.

As William Shakespeare eloquently stated in Romeo and Juliet, "A rose by any other name would smell as sweet." Ultimately, the label we attach to it is not as important as the essence it carries. Leading with meaning and purpose is a fundamental prerequisite for exemplary leadership and the achievement of extraordinary outcomes. What truly matters for leaders is harnessing this foundational leadership competency, as it has the power to transform both their leadership and their lives.

Discovering personal meaning and purpose necessitates asking tough questions of ourselves. Who am I? Why am I here? What deeply held beliefs guide me? What principles define my path? What keeps me grounded and focused? Finding answers to these challenging questions can be uncomfortable and time-consuming. However, the rewards are immeasurable.

Why start with why?

Let's consider the case of John, a senior vice-president who earnestly endeavors to lead effectively. Despite his efforts, he and his team continually face stagnant revenue growth, slightly declining engagement scores and productivity, and retention challenges. Stress levels are high, and John is not getting the rest he needs. He has attempted various strategies but is at a loss for what else to do.

One aspect he hasn't considered is leading with greater meaning and purpose. He has yet to pause and reflect on his own purpose and how it connects to his team and organization. He lacks a set of personal core values, a life mission, or a leadership philosophy that he actively practices, embodies, and lives by. No one has taught him how to leverage these essential elements.

Unfortunately, John is not alone. Many leaders today share similar stories. Let's explore a few reasons why leading with meaning and purpose is critical for leaders today.

A prerequisite to leadership

The first reason is that leading with meaning and purpose is a foundational prerequisite competency for leadership. In their book "Neuroscience for Leaders," Nikolaos Dimitriadis and Alexandros Psychogios emphasize the critical importance of leading with meaning and purpose. They state, "A higher purpose is not a leadership luxury but a leadership prerequisite."[2] Most leaders find themselves in management or leadership roles due to their exceptional performance as frontline contributors. Unfortunately, most organizations do not prioritize leadership development, let alone the foundational competency of leading with meaning and purpose. It's akin to enrolling in an advanced trigonometry or calculus class in high school without having first mastered simple algebra.

While leading with meaning and purpose is necessary, it is not sufficient. Leadership encompasses a broad spectrum of skills and competencies. However, without this foundational competency, all other competencies and outcomes will suffer.

Inside-Out

Another reason meaning and purpose are crucial for leaders is that humans are intrinsically wired for it. They are key to self-actualization, effective living, and human flourishing. According to Abraham Maslow, the father of Being Psychology, self-actualized individuals are devoted to causes beyond themselves. They work towards something that is precious to them—a calling or vocation that fate has somehow beckoned them to pursue.[3] While these individuals are focused on changing the world outside of themselves, their drive and passion stem from deep within.

Meaning and purpose also feature prominently in Steven R. Covey's book "The 7 Habits of Highly Effective People." Covey's second habit, "Begin with the End in Mind," centers on life purpose and the development of a Life Mission Statement. He suggests that we use our imagination to envision who we want to become and our conscience to determine the principles and values that will guide us. He refers to these as "true north" principles based on a character ethic.[4]

Covey expands on this concept in his subsequent book, "The 8th Habit," which calls for living from the inside-out rather than the outside-in. He explains the eighth habit as "Find Your Voice and Inspire Others to Find Theirs."[5]

Nearly 50 years ago, Victor Frankl founded logotherapy on the premise that our primary motivation is to find meaning or purpose in life.[6] More recently, Marty Seligman, the father of positive psychology, identified purpose as one of the core elements of human flourishing.[7] Success, according to modern psychology, emerges from character and a sense of personal significance, purpose, and meaning—not merely from personality, skills, techniques, or external motivators like bonuses or well-being programs.

The most successful and self-actualized individuals and leaders embark on a journey to find and develop their own unique meaning and purpose. Clarity regarding one's purpose leads to the highest levels of success and a profound sense of fulfillment.

Instead of success stemming from personality, skills, techniques, a positive attitude, or the old carrot and stick paradigm of management and leadership, success is born from character and a unique personal significance, purpose, and meaning.

That doesn't mean that other factors don't matter. They do. It's just that they are not the prime or foundational drivers of success. This is consistent with modern psychology. It is internal motivation that drives commitment and is the means to increasing motivation and productivity, not external motivators, like bonuses or wellbeing programs. Those certainly help, but they are not the primary drivers.

This is what the most successful and self-actualized people and leaders do. They find and develop their own unique meaning and purpose. Having clarity of yours will lead to the highest levels of success and a profound level of fulfillment.

Positive Connections & Wellbeing

Research demonstrates that individuals who perceive their lives as meaningful—with a clear sense of purpose—enjoy stronger personal relationships, experience fewer physical health problems, exhibit improved mental health, and adopt healthier lifestyles. Prominent well-being and human flourishing researchers Ed Diener and Marty Seligman report that people with high levels of well-being are more effective in various aspects of life. They are more likely to have successful relationships, be productive at work, earn higher incomes, and enjoy better physical and mental health.[8]

Impacts Key Business Metrics

Leading with meaning and purpose affects a wide range of business outcomes and metrics. According to Great Place to Work and numerous studies, organizations that fail to prioritize meaning and purpose experience lower levels of engagement, productivity, profitability, revenue, retention, and innovation. In contrast, purpose is a central focus for the 100 Best Companies to Work For, which consistently outperform those that do not prioritize meaning and purpose on all of these key metrics.[9]

Korn Ferry reports that nearly 70% of executive leaders believe that an organization's commitment to purpose-driven leadership significantly impacts long-term financial benefits, while individuals who embrace their organization's mission and purpose experience increased productivity.[10]

Overall Leadership Effectiveness.

Perhaps the most important outcome of all is that leaders who lead with meaning and purpose are simply more effective. Leaders who possess a clear leadership philosophy score higher on factors such as pride in their organization, commitment to their organization's success, willingness to exert effort, and overall effectiveness compared to those who lack clarity in their philosophy.

Furthermore, individuals working under leaders with a clear leadership philosophy report a stronger sense of team spirit, increased pride in their organization, a greater willingness to invest time and effort, and the feeling of making a meaningful difference. Notably, these individuals rate their leaders 140% higher on the statement "Overall, my supervisor is an effective leader" compared to leaders with low clarity of philosophy.[11]

Given the numerous positive outcomes associated with leading with meaning and purpose, it is vital for leaders to consider it a personal and business imperative. By embracing this approach, leaders can unlock their full potential, inspire their teams, and achieve meaningful and sustainable success.

What is a leadership philosophy?

As a leader, people look to you for inspiration, guidance, empowerment, and vision. They seek to determine if you walk the talk and embody the qualities you espouse. In essence, they are asking, "Do you talk the talk?" and "Can you walk the talk?" Leading with meaning and purpose starts with you.

If we envision leadership and life as a journey, embarking on that journey without a destination, compass, roadmap, or any form of guidance is akin to just wandering aimlessly.

A leadership philosophy is a statement that outlines why and how a leader leads. It encompasses a set of principles, beliefs, and core values that guide and direct behavior. It enhances self-awareness, influences how a leader perceives the world and evaluates information, and empowers them to make effective and courageous decisions. A leadership philosophy also shapes how leaders interact with people, events, and situations, inspiring both themselves and others. Additionally, it serves as a tool for seeking and integrating feedback on leadership style and behaviors.

The purpose of a leadership philosophy is to provide clarity and consistency in a leader's actions, serving as a foundation for building a positive and effective leadership culture. Its strength lies in its ability to help leaders remain focused on their purpose, maintain their integrity, and create an environment where individuals can thrive and collectively achieve goals in the face of adversity and change.

A leadership philosophy should genuinely, clearly, and categorically define what you believe in as both a person and a leader. It should illuminate how you lead at your best, articulate your personal purpose, mission, vocation, or passion, and serve as an operating system for making a positive difference in the world.

What's the secret sauce?

- A. P. J. Abdul Kalam, the renowned Indian aerospace scientist and former president of India, eloquently encapsulated my approach to working with leaders in his Four Beautiful Thoughts of Life:

- B. *Look back and get experience.*

    Look forward and see hope.

    Look around and find reality.

    Look within and find yourself.

These profound words align with my methodology when assisting leaders who aspire to unlock the immense power of a leadership philosophy. I have further expanded on these ideas in my comprehensive and engaging online course, "Leading with Meaning & Purpose." By delving into each of these thoughts, you will unlock your full leadership potential.

Look back and get experience.

This element invites you to reflect on past experiences and identify and clarify core values and principles. By examining your decisions, actions, and outcomes, you can discern patterns and gain valuable insights that align with your core values and principles. This element addresses the question, "Who am I?" from a historical perspective.

Look forward and see hope.

Envisioning a future that transcends mere success and taps into a deeper sense of meaning and purpose, allows you to set more meaningful goals and objectives that are rooted in your higher cause or purpose. This element answers the question, "Why am I here?"

Look around and find reality.

Assess your current state as both a leader and an individual. Examine your strengths, weaknesses, and opportunities for improvement. Understand the dynamics of your team and the broader organizational context. By comprehending your present reality, you can identify areas for growth and development, enabling informed decisions and driving positive change. This provides a current-state response to the question, "Who am I?"

Look within and find yourself.

Emphasize self-awareness and personal growth as vital for leadership. Leaders who understand their own strengths, weaknesses, values, and beliefs are better equipped to lead authentically and build trust with their teams. This element encourages deep introspection, completing the answer to who you are.

By integrating these elements into your leadership philosophy, you can cultivate a more authentic and purpose-driven approach. This fosters personal growth, inspires your team, and ultimately enables you to achieve meaningful and sustainable success.

Remember, you became a leader to make a difference in the world. This necessitates a continual search for new ways to lead, developing strategies, acquiring resources, refining your vision, and establishing or revising goals. Make leading with greater meaning and purpose a core strategy of your leadership journey.

***

To contact Alan:

Phone: 346-291-0216

email: alan@alanmikolaj.com

Website: https://www.alanmikolaj.com/

LinkedIn: https://www.linkedin.com/in/alan-mikolaj/

The Leading with Meaning & Purpose Developmental Experience:

https://www.alanmikolaj.com/the-course.html

References

[1] Schwantes, M. (2019, May 27). Warren Buffett says he became a self-made billionaire because he played by 1 simple rule of life (which most people don't). Inc.com.

[2] Dimitriadis, N., & Psychogios, A. (2016). Neuroscience for Leaders: A brain adaptive leadership approach. Kogan Page Publishers.

[3] Maslow, A. H. (1971). The Farther Reaches of Human Nature. Arkana/Penguin Books.

[4] Covey, S. R. (2004). The 7 habits of Highly Effective People: Restoring the character ethic ([Rev. ed.].). New York: Free Press.

[5] Covey, Stephen R. (2004). The 8th Habit: From effectiveness to greatness. New York: Free Press.

[6] Frankl, V. E. (1992). Man's Search for Meaning: An introduction to logotherapy (4th ed.) (I. Lasch, Trans.). Beacon Press.

[7] Seligman, M. E. P. (2011). Flourish: A visionary new understanding of happiness and well-being. Free Press.

[8] Diener, E., & Seligman, M. E. (2004). Beyond money: Toward an economy of well-being. Psychological Science in the Public Interest, 5(1), 1-31.

[9] Bush, M. & Great Place to Work. (2023, April 4). The Fortune 100 Best Companies prove that caring for employees and increasing productivity can go hand in hand. Fortune.

[10] Korn Ferry. (2016, June 8). Korn Ferry executive survey: Where there's purpose, there's profit. Korn Ferry Institute.

[11] Kouzes, J. & Posner, B. (2017). The Leadership Challenge: How to make extraordinary things happen in organizations (6th ed.). John Wiley & Sons, Inc.

Amanda Irtz

Amanda Irtz is the founder and CEO of Confident Parent Collective, LLC a renowned authority in the field of parenting and family support. With a deep passion for empowering families, she has dedicated her life's work to being the guiding light for those seeking confidence, connection, and fulfillment in their parenting journey.

As a best-selling author, Amanda has penned two influential books. *The Clouds That Chase Us: A Journey into Autism* offers a heartfelt exploration of her personal experiences navigating the world of autism. In *Launch the Legacy: Creating a Business Brand That Builds Generational Wealth*, she shares her expertise, creating a legacy and successful business.

Amanda cherishes her role as a mother to two incredible children who bring both laughter and tears to her life. Drawing from her own experiences as a parent, she brings an authentic and relatable perspective to her work.

Prior to her career in writing and parenting advocacy, Amanda Irtz spent 22 years in education, serving as both a teacher and a school administrator. This experience laid the foundation for her understanding of the challenges and joys of raising children while juggling the demands of modern life.

Residing in the Colorado Rockies, Amanda finds solace and inspiration in the natural beauty that surrounds her. She enjoys daily Pilates workouts and walks with her dogs, nurturing both her physical and mental well-being.

Restoring Wholeness: Unearthing the Beautiful Truths in Parenting

by Amanda Irtz

Tired eyes look at the numbers on the microwave. It reads 5:30 AM. I don't like this time of day because it is dark – and I want to be in bed when it is dark. However, I've learned that getting out of bed early (and quietly) is my only salvation for the day. I find my quiet spot in my mustard-yellow velvet chair and prepare for a few moments of morning meditation. I'm not talking about meditation that takes an hour. No, the morning meditation that I squeeze into my day takes about 11 minutes (tops). Eleven minutes for me and whatever mantra I choose to focus on for the day--eleven minutes to get myself prepared for the day ahead.

Somewhere between the mantras "I am love" and "I create my own miracles," I feel the quintessential small hands on my feet. The hands stay rested on my feet until I open my eyes to the strawberry-blonde boy before me. Using his hands, he motions to his stomach and then creates a chomping motion with his mouth. I motion back with two open fists, knowing very well that my meditation is over, and I must scramble into mommy mode.

Why was I destined to navigate the path of single motherhood? Overwhelmed by judgmental glances when I couldn't perfectly handle a tantrum, I doubted my mothering abilities. Juggling the demands of getting my children to school and punctually reaching my school, where I served as an assistant principal, left me feeling like I was failing on all fronts. Why was it such a struggle to balance friendships, relationships, idyllic vacations, and weekend escapes? Why couldn't I live the life I yearned for while being the parent I knew I could be?

Yes, why?

After years of silent crying and fear of what others would think, I made a bold realization. I love my children. Period. And I am not showing them my true love by living my life in constant fear of what others think. I am not a victim of my life. I am blessed.

So, I shattered that restrictive shell to pieces and let my heart radiate with love. Truly, the more I loved my son and daughter for everything and all they were, the less the fear trickled into my life. I also learned to appreciate my unique awesomeness and celebrate my achievements, however small. I found strength in my flaws and realized they were what made me human, relatable, and authentic. This journey taught me that my mistakes or shortcomings do not define my worth but my resilience and ability to overcome them. Thus, my why turned into a big, flashy sign with neon lights. Honestly, my why was my calling for this journey called parenting. My *why* was, and still is, about not just being a good mother but living my most extraordinary life, too.

My why wasn't a glaring, theatrical alarm. Instead, it was like a snooze button that I continued hitting repeatedly until I finally woke up. I discovered myself losing out on invaluable moments with my children—moments I could never find again. From the morning embraces to the spur-of-the-moment dance-offs in our living room and even the classic tantrums over a misplaced favorite pair of turquoise pants—these occurrences were increasingly disappearing. This was happening amidst my ceaseless efforts to balance the hefty responsibility of supporting over 500 students and their families at my school while simultaneously aiming to mold my children into a better version than the one they were presently observing in me.

The constant stress started to take a toll on my health. My sleep became sporadic and restless, and my appetite dwindled. My body, resilient as it was, couldn't keep up with the relentless pace and began to show signs of shutting down. Some might label this as burnout—a term often used to describe the emotional, physical, and mental exhaustion caused by prolonged stress. But I prefer to see it differently. I chose to view it not as a dead-end but as an opportunity—a chance to pivot.

This 'pivot' wasn't about making a complete U-turn or abandoning everything I had created. Instead, it represented a conscious shift in my approach towards parenting and life. It meant prioritizing my well-being, setting boundaries, and, most importantly, allowing myself the grace to be imperfect.

Transitioning into my new role as a Parenting Coach was a natural progression that stemmed from my deep-rooted passion for supporting families and children, which I had nurtured during my time within the school system. Drawing from the chapters of my life, I recognized the importance of listening more than speaking, understanding each family's unique dynamics, and communicating effectively with parents. This understanding became the cornerstone of my coaching approach. I committed to a rigorous certification process, immersing myself in child development and psychology studies. This academic foundation, coupled with my first-hand experiences, equipped me to navigate familial issues and provide evidence-based strategies.

However, my journey was about more than just gaining credentials or learning techniques. It was about staying true to my mission and being open to new possibilities. It was about acknowledging that becoming a Parenting Coach wasn't just a career change but a life priority. In my new role, my passion didn't feel like work. Instead, it felt like a purpose-driven path closely tied to my core values. I was finally able to create the balance I sought, not just in my life but also in the lives of the families I worked with.

And so, I launched my parent coach business, the Confident Parent Collective, with the mission of creating a world where all parents are happy, healthy, and whole. My goal was simple:

- Help parents understand their strengths.
- Improve their communication.
- Create nurturing environments for their children.

In doing so, I realized that my shift wasn't just about supporting families outside the school system but also about empowering them to navigate the exciting, terrifying, and humbling parenting process.

So, how did I shift into this place? This new knowledge? Well, it happened during the many moments sitting in my mustard-yellow velvet chair in the dark morning hours. It happened when I told myself I needed to focus on the joy in my life, release worn-out expectations, and commit to loving myself in every moment.

Focus on the Joy

Now, I willingly admit that I don't focus on the joy every moment—or even every day. I know I should look for the joy in the meltdowns over a missing Lego piece, the turkey bacon being too cold, or my cup of coffee spilling down the front of my blouse. There has to be joy in our day-to-day moments, right?

And when these not-so-joyful moments occur, I often start a story in my mind. It usually sounds like, "My life is so hard, and there are no breaks, and how will things ever change?" My negative story can grow and change into a bigger beast by hyper-focusing on just one small aspect of my day. When I tell myself that "no one hears my voice in meetings," that reality often starts growing in my life.

Your negative story may differ from mine, but we all have these inside voices that repeatedly tell us stories. Maybe your negative story is about using the wrong words or coming across as too brash or clumsy.

I will also admit that shifting my negative story into a joyful one is challenging. However, I do try. I try to ask myself, *What if there were something to be joyful about? Is there any joy here in this story?*

Let's look a bit deeper into my **negative story**: Why can't my life be easier? Why do I have to be so responsible for everything – the bills, the groceries, the love, the discipline, and plunging the clogged toilet? I'm so tired. I feel like all I do is give and give – and then I collapse at night. Is that what my life is destined to be?

It's not a very inspiring and motivating story, right? And really, who wants to hear such a story?

Now, let's go deeper and dig out some of the joy. Again, I will note that this is not easy work for me either. However, the more I try, the better at it I become. My **joy-filled story:** My life is overflowing with opportunities and love. My kids are never bored because they are involved in so many activities – and I know this adds richness and texture to their stories. I know they are happy because of their constant giggling. And I am a jack of all trades! Who can really say

THAT about themselves? I mean honestly: Mom, Parenting Coach, Kid Chauffeur, Toilet Un-clogger, Battery Replacer, Expert Lego Finder, and Knower of All (according to my kids) Bam! And, the beginning of a new day is my reminder that life is my constant teacher – and that it is better to be tired and filled with love than to have nothing at all.

The negative story often revolves around feeling overwhelmed by life's challenges. The joy-filled story, on the other hand, focuses on the opportunities these challenges present. It celebrates love, resilience, and the power of being a versatile parent.

I've learned that where we put our energy determines what grows in our lives. If we focus on the negative, it will consume us. But if we direct our energy towards finding joy and growth, even in the smallest moments, we'll start to see change.

Being a parent is tough; there's no denying that. But instead of letting the difficulties define our story, we can see them as opportunities for growth. By doing so, we not only become better parents, but we also find joy in the journey.

So, here are some thoughts to reflect on:

What negative stories are you telling yourself? Can you rewrite them with a more positive, joy-focused narrative?

How can you turn your challenges into opportunities for growth?

Where are you putting your energy? Is it fostering joy or feeding negativity?

Release Worn-out Expectations

I found myself clinging to tired, worn-out expectations that were more fantasy than reality. Here are some of the beliefs I once held as gospel:

My children's emotions (whether they were angry, joyful, sad, etc.) directly reflected my parenting skills. I believed their feelings were a mirror reflecting the effectiveness or shortcomings of my efforts as a parent.

Parenting was nothing more than a checklist of tasks and logistics to be delivered on a daily basis. It seemed like a never-ending conveyor belt of duties, chores, and responsibilities, leaving little room for spontaneity or joy.

Family dinners had to always be at the table with every member present. This image of family harmoniously gathered around the dinner table became an inflexible rule rather than a flexible guideline.

I was somehow bound by an unwritten, sacred parenting law to be present and accounted for at every activity my kids were involved in, as if my absence would somehow irrevocably damage their development.

When I stepped back and examined these self-created expectations, I asked myself a simple yet profound question: How did these expectations make me feel? The words that flowed onto the paper were sobering:

- Failure
- Anxious
- Exhausted

Full stop. This is not what parenting is about. This is not what life is about. I certainly don't want my children ever to experience these feelings in their lives, let alone daily. It was here that I decided to take out the trash, metaphorically speaking. I decided to toss out these worn-out expectations that were weighing me down. I said, no more.

Now it's your turn. I invite you to reflect on your expectations. Remember, it's okay to reassess and let go of expectations not serving you or your family's happiness and well-being.

What expectations of parenting or life are you holding onto that may be more of a fantasy than reality?

Are there any beliefs you hold as absolute truths that might be causing you more stress than peace?

How does viewing parenting as a checklist of tasks affect your ability to find joy in the process?

Are there any routines or traditions (like family dinners) that you've made inflexible rules in your life? How might loosening these rules create more room for joy and spontaneity?

Do you feel obligated to be present for every single one of your child's activities? How might reassessing this expectation alleviate some pressure?

Take a moment to write down how your current expectations make you feel. Are these feelings aligning with the life and parenting experience you want to have?

What worn-out expectations are you ready to toss to create more room for joy, spontaneity, and overall well-being?

Commit to Loving Myself

Learning to love myself was one of the most challenging and transformative aspects of my journey toward discovering my true parenting power and rekindling my zest for life. And by this, I mean genuinely embracing and cherishing who I am – in all the messy, hairy moments as well as the glittering, sparkly ones.

There was a time when I'd berate myself for being two minutes late to pick up my kids. But part of loving myself means letting go of such stringent self-criticism. It means understanding that perfection is unattainable and that it's okay to make mistakes. It means acknowledging that I am human and that sometimes, things won't go as planned, and that's perfectly alright.

Loving myself also reshaped my identity. It shifted my role from someone who always needed to be right to someone who was vulnerable and curious. This didn't mean I was weak or indecisive; it was about being open to new experiences, opinions, and perspectives. It was about asking questions, seeking knowledge, and understanding that there's always room for growth and improvement.

This journey of self-love led me to reconnect with a version of myself that I hadn't seen since I was 18 years old. It was like rediscovering a long-lost friend, hidden beneath layers of societal expectations, parental responsibilities, and self-doubt. It was exhilarating and liberating.

But let me clarify: Loving myself goes beyond indulging in a bubble bath or savoring a cup of tea – although those self-care moments are also essential. It's about embarking on a relentless quest to discover the parts of me that truly matter. It's about recognizing my worth and understanding that I deserve love and kindness, especially from myself.

So, here's my message to you: Loving yourself is an ongoing journey, not a destination. It's about embracing who you are, flaws and all, and acknowledging that you are enough, just as you are. And remember, your ability to love and care for others is deeply connected to your capacity to love and care for yourself. So, embark on this quest of self-discovery and self-love, and watch as it transforms not just your parenting but your entire life. Are you ready to reflect on your self-love? Here are some guiding questions for you:

How would you describe your relationship with yourself at this moment? Is there room for more self-love and acceptance?

Can you recall a recent instance where you were overly critical of yourself? How could a more self-loving perspective change that narrative?

How comfortable are you with showing vulnerability? Do you see it as a strength or a weakness?

Can you identify parts of yourself that you've lost touch with over the years? What steps can you take to reconnect with those aspects?

What are some ways you can begin to love and accept yourself more, especially in times of mistakes and imperfections?

In what ways can you show more kindness and compassion to yourself on a daily basis?

Reminder: it's a journey of self-discovery, and your path will look different. The important thing is to start the journey and stay committed to it.

As we conclude this chapter, let's revisit the moment I sat in my mustard-yellow velvet chair, meditating and seeking guidance. I was grappling with expectations, self-doubt, and the pressures of parenting. But if you've journeyed with me through this chapter, you'll see that I – and, by extension, you – have the power to turn things around.

If you're feeling lost or overwhelmed like I once did, my advice to you is: Pause. Breathe. Reflect. You are not alone. We all stumble, falter, and struggle. But remember, in these moments of struggle, we often find our greatest strength.

Understand that transforming your parenting, and in turn, your life, is a process. It's not a switch that can be flipped overnight. It requires patience, self-compassion, and, most importantly, a commitment to loving yourself through every high and low. It means releasing worn-out expectations, embracing vulnerability, and rediscovering parts of yourself that the demands of life and parenting have overshadowed.

But here's the most beautiful part: You can do it. You have the power to change, grow, and become the best version of yourself, not just as a parent but as an individual. Remember, the words "I can" are powerful. Repeat them to yourself. Believe in them because the first step to any transformation starts with believing it's possible.

So, as you close this chapter and move forward, carry these reflections and insights with you. Use them as tools to navigate your journey. And no matter how challenging things may seem, never lose sight of the hope that sparked your quest for change.

Because just like me, you too can find your true parenting power and zest for life. You, too, can turn things around. You, too, can create a life filled with joy, fulfillment, and self-love. And that journey starts now.

***

To contact Amanda:

https://confidentparentcollective.com

https://linktr.ee/amandairtz

Tra Urban

Tra Urban, known as the "Medicine Woman," is an internationally acclaimed healer, transformational teacher, and best-selling author. Her journey of personal empowerment and healing has inspired countless individuals worldwide to discover their innate potential and purpose.

Tra's path to becoming a renowned healer was marked by a life-altering car accident in 2010 that left her paralyzed. However, this pivotal moment led her to a profound spiritual awakening and a relentless pursuit of her true purpose. Through years of self-discovery, intensive healing, and learning from wisdom keepers and healers worldwide, she developed a deep understanding of energy, perception, and the mind-body-spirit connection.

Today, Tra offers a range of transformational courses, healing sessions, and workshops designed to empower individuals to heal themselves and create lives aligned with their purpose. She has authored the internationally acclaimed book "Healthapedia" and is a sought-after speaker on topics of healing, abundance, and personal empowerment. Tra's vision is to create a world where everyone can live in harmony with their true selves, tapping into their limitless potential for well-being and abundance.

Unlocking Life's Secrets ~ A Journey of Personal Empowerment

By Tra Urban

I invite you to share a remarkable journey with me, one marked by transformation, resilience, and boundless potential for change—a journey to inspire with valuable lessons about personal empowerment and living a better life.

Imagine a moment in your life when you felt an urgent need for change, even though you may not have known exactly what or how that change would come about. That's precisely how I felt before the most profound turning point in my life.

In 2010, a life-altering car accident left me paralyzed, but the root of my journey stretches further back. Leaving home at 15, I dropped out of school and became a mother of three by age 19. My marriage to Ben, though instructive, did not provide the answers I sought. I prayed for purpose, unaware of what lay ahead.

I possessed the gift of rapid manifestation, but it often led me astray. My life was a whirlwind of commitments, helping others while neglecting self-care. One day, watching TV with Ben, I noticed a recurring theme of gratitude. It was a sign, an answer to my plea for guidance.

In the months preceding my life-changing accident, my schedule overflowed with obligations like my daughter and friend's weddings, committee meetings, church group responsibilities, and a demanding workload. I was perpetually engaged, ready to help, teach, and empower others to achieve their goals. This, I later realized, was a gift I hadn't yet applied to my own life. Self-care and self-love remained elusive lessons until everything began to unravel.

Then came the day that would alter my life's course. Our car was rear ended, leaving me with a spinal injury that required emergency surgery. It was a definite reminder to pay attention to life's signs and confront my inner dissatisfaction.

As my journey unfolded, I began to understand the interconnectedness of our emotional, mental, and spiritual bodies. The emotional body records experiences through our senses, while the mental body, often referred to as the ego, can limit us with doubts and beliefs. The spiritual body, our subconscious, connects us to the divine and our limitless potential.

I delved deeper, discovering the distinction between ground causes and root causes. Ground causes are recurring, problematic cycles triggered by the root cause. Seeking help from professionals, I realized that talk therapy often only addresses ground causes, allowing issues to resurface in different forms. Western medicine, too, keeps treatment at the surface level, ignoring the roots that continue to manifest in various ways.

My insight was clear: our thoughts and feelings about ourselves—the root cause—manifest as external symptoms. This understanding led to a profound realization that our perception shapes our reality. By shifting our perspective and taking ownership of our experiences, we gain the power to rewrite the narrative of our lives.

I believe life is always perfect and aligned with what serves our highest good. Our souls seek elevation through education, and until we grasp the lesson and make a change, trauma will persist. The Law of Attraction operates not out of intelligence, but obedience to energy. To effect change, we must capture every thought and heed its lesson.

Owning our experiences places us in a position to rewrite the story. Everything in life is perception, and when we perceive things differently, outcomes change—a principle rooted in simple quantum physics.

What if you shifted your perspective to believe that every experience, both good and bad, was preparing you for the grand life you're destined to live? This shift in perception is the key to leveraging every moment of impact, transforming you from a defensive player into an offensive all-star, calling your own plays and leading life on your terms.

In a world of unexpected transitions, it's crucial to continuously assess, re-strategize, and adapt. Perception, if you're open to it, can always change. As long as we have time on this earth, there are opportunities to grow, learn, and ascend. Our greatest ability lies in the power of our minds and emotions to create and manifest whatever captures our focus.

I encourage you to leverage every moment in your life, tap into and unpack your programmed thoughts and buried emotions. Then, ask yourself, "How can I transmute my experiences into the joy that fills my cup?" Remember, dear reader, the journey towards personal empowerment and a better life begins with a shift in perception and a willingness to learn and grow.

Now, let's explore how this journey began, what I'm doing now, and my vision for the future.

Navigating Life's Unforeseen Turns

The immediate aftermath of the accident was a whirlwind of emotions and adaptations. Over the course of those initial 30 days, I found myself grappling with the fundamentals of daily life in a new and unfamiliar way. Everyday tasks that had once been second nature, such as ascending a flight of stairs or entering and exiting a car, were now monumental challenges. It was during these early days of adjustment that I began to truly explore the depths of my own resilience and self-discovery.

Just a few months prior to the chaos and uncertainty, I believe Divinely orchestrated, an unexpected beacon of hope emerged—my introduction to "The Secret." This revelation opened my eyes to the extraordinary potential of healing and transformation that lay within each of us.

One particular story from "The Secret" struck a chord deep within me—a narrative of a man whose body had been shattered from head to toe. Despite dire prognoses, he defied all odds and, against all expectations, walked out of the hospital by Christmas. This remarkable account became a source of inspiration, reinforcing my belief in the immense power of the mind and spirit to surmount even the most daunting challenges.

My journey took an even more profound turn as I delved into the realm of holistic healing. I encountered Reiki practitioners and shamanic mentors from diverse corners of the world, each imparting their unique wisdom and insights. These encounters broadened my understanding of energy healing and illuminated the intricate interplay between the mind, body, and spirit.

My thirst for knowledge led me to connect with Native American indigenous healers and wisdom keepers, tapping into my own Native American ancestry. I underwent healing sessions and gained wisdom from healers spanning the globe, including Pygmy Tribal medicine practitioners from Australia. These encounters honed my innate healing abilities, eventually earning me the moniker "Medicine Woman".

Through these experiences, I realized that every individual possesses a unique healing recipe and a personal reset button to thrive and embrace their best life. Witnessing stage 4 cancer patients achieve remission without chemotherapy, individuals with diabetes transform their health, and countless others finding renewed purpose and vitality affirmed this revelation.

My journey instilled in me a profound belief that life unfolds perfectly in alignment with our highest good. It underscored the importance of embracing life's lessons and facilitating transformative change to break the cycle of trauma. The Law of Attraction, I understood, wasn't driven by intelligence but by energy, obediently responding to our energetic frequencies. It was only by capturing and integrating the wisdom of every thought that we could effect profound shifts in our lives.

For years, I embarked on a transformative odyssey, traveling alongside Native tribal chiefs and actively participating in sacred ceremonies. My journey also extended to the digital realm, where I live-streamed and meticulously documented these profound events, sharing the invaluable teachings and insights with a global audience. However, as the world's circumstances evolved, my travels faced an abrupt interruption. The passing of many revered tribal chiefs and the unforeseen challenges of covid changing world necessitated a pivot in my path.

So, what if we shifted our perspective to view every experience—both positive and negative—as preparation for the grand life we're destined to lead? This shift in perception held the key to leveraging every moment of impact, transitioning from a defensive player to an offensive all-star, and calling our own plays in the game of life.

In the face of these unforeseen trials, I chose to embrace change and express gratitude for the fresh opportunities that presented themselves. This journey led me to Clubhouse—a dynamic platform where I encountered a vibrant tribe of kindred spirits, from diverse backgrounds and walks of life. Together, we support one another's endeavors, and collectively work towards elevating our shared consciousness.

This abbreviated exploration merely scratches the surface of the transformative power of adaptability and the pursuit of wisdom from a multitude of sources. It serves as a testament to the profound impact of embracing life's unexpected twists and uncovering new avenues for growth, enlightenment, and ascension.

I invite you to embrace every moment in your life, unravel the programmed thoughts and buried emotions that shape your reality, and ask yourself: "How can I transmute my experiences into the joy that fills my cup?" This is where personal empowerment and a better life truly begin—a shift in perception and a wholehearted commitment to growth.

Let's explore my ongoing endeavors, and my vision for the future.

Propelling Forward Motion

My journey is a testament to the transformative power of energy and perception. It's a journey that has traversed the depths of personal healing, the heights of enlightenment, and the boundless potential of human existence. Today, I am not just a witness to this journey but a guide for others seeking their path to empowerment and self-discovery.

At this juncture of my adventure, my focus is on sharing my insights and expertise with those who are ready to harness the remarkable forces of energy and perception. My courses are the cornerstone of this endeavor, designed to illuminate the path towards personal transformation, empowerment, and the fulfillment of one's potential.

As an internationally recognized healer, I am committed to sharing my gifts and wisdom with a global audience. One of the ways I do this is through my free Healing Hands Masterclass, designed for individuals who work with their hands. This immersive experience allows participants to understand how they absorb energy and gain practical tools to cleanse and align their energetic field. By empowering them to become aware of the energy they carry, I help them step into their full potential as healers.

In the realm of energy mastery, my curriculum extends beyond tiers and structures. It is a tapestry of knowledge and wisdom, each thread representing a unique facet of personal growth and self-realization. Among these threads, I offer courses that explore energy awareness, application, and mastery. These courses serve as a compass for individuals seeking to navigate the intricate landscapes of their inner worlds.

But my journey is not confined to the realm of energy alone. It extends into the realm of holistic well-being and the recognition of the interconnectedness of all living beings. This recognition has led to the development of a unique offering—my Pet Reset program.

For pet owners grappling with their beloved companions' unwanted behaviors, the Pet Reset program serves as a lifeline. It delves into the profound connection between trapped emotions and pet behavior, offering solutions and guidance for restoring harmony between pets and their owners. Through this program, pet owners can embark on a journey of healing and understanding, nurturing the bond they share with their four-legged friends.

But what sets this journey apart is not just the courses and programs; it's the community that surrounds it. The Empower Hour, a weekly gathering, stands as a testament to the power of collective growth and support. It is a space where individuals come together to share their experiences, insights, and challenges. In this community, healing is not a solitary endeavor but a collective journey towards empowerment and self-discovery.

In addition to my role as an educator, I stand as an author—a conduit for knowledge and transformation. The collaborative book, "Healthapedia," has achieved the remarkable distinction of becoming a number one bestseller in thirteen countries. This international acclaim underscores the universal hunger for wisdom and healing, a hunger that transcends borders and cultures.

While the world faced a momentary pause due to the pandemic I found new avenues for growth and connection through platforms like Clubhouse where I support, motivate, educate and empower 6 days a week—a space where kindred spirits converge to support and uplift each other.

Furthermore, I lead interactive workshops on landing pages and sales funnels, providing individuals with the knowledge and skills they need to monetize their unique products or services. My aim is to demystify the world of online marketing, making it accessible to those who wish to share their gifts with the world.

My journey is not defined by a destination but by a continuous unfolding—a relentless pursuit of understanding, healing, and empowerment. It's a journey that thrives on the exchange of knowledge, the power of community, and the recognition of our limitless potential.

As I stand at this juncture of my journey, I am filled with a sense of purpose and fulfillment. My mission is clear—to guide individuals towards their own paths of empowerment, healing, and self-discovery. The journey is ongoing, and the road ahead is illuminated by the collective desire for growth and transformation.

In the next chapter, we will explore the vision that propels me forward—a vision of a world where individuals are empowered to recognize their true worth, align with their purpose, and manifest their desires with clarity and intention. Together, we embark on a journey of limitless potential, where the boundaries of reality are defined only by the scope of our imagination and the depth of our understanding.

Vision of Expansive Potential

As I cast my gaze upon the horizon, envisioning a world bathed in the radiant glow of harmony and well-being. This vision is not just a dream; it is a profound belief rooted in the transformative power of energy, perception, and the unwavering connection between all living beings. In this final chapter, we embark on a journey of exploration—a journey into the realm of vision, where the boundaries of reality are defined only by the scope of our imagination and the depth of our understanding.

My vision, dear one, is a tapestry woven with threads of empowerment, healing, and expansive potential. It is a vision that encompasses not just individuals but the collective consciousness of humanity—a vision where each thought, each word, and each action ripples through the fabric of existence, shaping a world in perfect alignment with our collective desires.

At the core of this vision lies a fundamental truth—an understanding that we are all interconnected, bound together by the invisible threads of energy and consciousness. In this intricate web of existence, every thought carries weight, every emotion has resonance, and every action reverberates through the tapestry of reality. It is this understanding that forms the foundation of my vision—a vision of a world where this profound interconnectedness is acknowledged and celebrated.

Imagine, for a moment, a world where every individual recognizes the power they hold within themselves—the power to shape their reality, to manifest their desires, and to create a life that resonates with their highest purpose. It is a world where the limitations of fear, doubt, and scarcity have given way to the boundless horizons of abundance, joy, and well-being.

In this world, the law of attraction is not just a concept but a way of life—an understanding that our thoughts are the architects of our reality. It is a world where individuals embrace the responsibility that comes with this knowledge, where they choose to focus on thoughts that align with health, abundance, and harmony. In doing so, they become conscious co-creators of a reality that mirrors their most cherished aspirations.

But my vision extends beyond the realm of personal empowerment. It reaches into the collective consciousness, where a global shift in perception has taken root. It is a shift that transcends borders, cultures, and divides—a shift that recognizes the inherent worth of every individual and the sanctity of all life.

In this vision, the challenges that plague our world find resolution not through external interventions but through a profound internal transformation. It is a transformation that occurs as humanity collectively embraces the truth that our thoughts are the genesis of our experiences. With this awareness, individuals and communities unite in a shared focus on health, abundance, and well-being, rendering issues of scarcity and lack obsolete.

It is a vision where empathy, compassion, and love are the guiding principles of human interaction—a world where conflicts are resolved through understanding, where differences are celebrated as sources of enrichment, and where every voice is heard and valued. It's a world where gratitude flows freely, where appreciation is the currency of exchange, and where acts of kindness are the cornerstones of society.

As I hold this vision, I am filled with a profound sense of gratitude. I give thanks each day for the privilege of sharing these insights, for the opportunity to guide others on their paths of empowerment and healing, and for the knowledge that our collective journey is one of expansive potential.

In closing, my vision is not a distant dream; it is a living, breathing reality that unfolds with each moment. It is a reality that you, dear one, have the power to co-create through your thoughts, your emotions, and your actions. As we traverse this journey of self-discovery and empowerment, may we do so with the knowledge that the world we envision is not a distant mirage but a tangible destination—a destination where harmony, well-being, and pure potential reign supreme.

Together, we embark on this remarkable journey—a journey that transcends time and space, a journey that leads us to the boundless shores of a harmonious world where all things are possible, and where the highest and greatest good of all is not just a vision but a living truth.

Thank you for joining me on this odyssey of transformation, empowerment, and vision. May your journey be illuminated by the radiant light of your expansive potential, and may you continue to manifest a world that resonates with the harmonious song of your heart.

***

To contact Tra:

WEBSITE

https://tratalk.net/

SOCIAL MEDIA

IG https://www.instagram.com/traurbanofficial/?hl=en

FB https://www.facebook.com/tratalk/

LinkedIn https://www.linkedin.com/in/traurban/

Tic/Tok https://www.tiktok.com/@traurban

EDUCATION

https://4bodiesofenergy.com/

https://healinghandsmasterclass.com/

SERVICES

Free https://claritycallwithtra.com/

https://empowerhourwithtra.com/

https://petresetnow.com/

https://releasebusinessblocks.com/

https://energysessionwithtra.com/

EVENTS

https://experienceelevatedentrepreneurs.com/

https://digintolandingpages.com/

PODCAST

https://digintobiz.com/

HEALTHAPEDIA BOOK

https://healthapediabook.com/

COURSES

https://energynme.com/

https://energynyou.com/

Victor Hailey

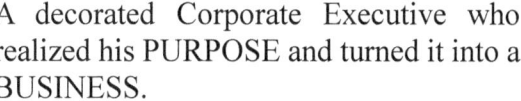

A decorated Corporate Executive who realized his PURPOSE and turned it into a BUSINESS.

WHY: Become the Best Version of my Self and Share that Gift with the World.

HOW: Addicted to Personal Growth and Changing the World.

WHAT: Coaching & Philanthropy.

I help business people find their TRUE self and achieve REAL success!

I've been called: Executive Coach, Financial Coach, Professional Coach, Purpose Coach, Performance Enhancement Coach, Life Coach, Habit Hacker, and much more. These titles are all fine by me. All I care about is delivering results.

In the spirit of generosity, 11.11% of client fees are donated, in their name, to 1 of 5 select charities, for a unique pay-it-forward business.

From Suffering to Hope: A Journey of Personal Development

By Victor Hailey

Act 1: THE SUFFERING

Little did I know that an embarrassing business lunch could lead to a lifetime of growth and possibility.

In the late '90s, as a young black man climbing the corporate ladder, the odds were stacked against me in a field dominated by those I did not resemble.

The Midwest corporate headquarters, adorned with gold-framed portraits of past corporate executives and board members, felt like a battleground of unfamiliar territory. Thick oil on canvas captured each with a head of white hair to match their white skin and blue blazers with gold buttons. I sensed the weight of their historical privilege, a sensation reminiscent of my mother's experience on the plantation where she was born and raised in the Deep South as a sharecropper. Walking these halls was akin to her walking into the "big house". The halls echoed the success stories of those who preceded us, their portraits watching over us, seemingly judging our every move. However, determined to overcome adversity as she demonstrated, I resolved to become the Victor, not the victim, living into my namesake.

In a few short years, with grit and confidence, I earned my spot amongst the best of the best. A corner office, company car, fancy title, high salary, annual bonuses, and award plaques illustrated my achievements.

It was during a crucial business lunch at an upscale eatery in Los Angeles that the tide turned. Seated across from a client I had been pursuing for over a year, I confidently secured a multi-million-dollar deal, landing the biggest piece of business in my career to date and toppling the incumbent agency. The deal was worth millions to our company's portfolio and came with some nice bragging rights. I was sitting on top of the world. I was doing cartwheels on the inside, while maintaining my cool, calm, and collected demeanor on the outside.

However, the sweet taste of victory turned bitter when the check arrived, I reached down in my pocket and I realized I had left my wallet at home on the bathroom counter.

Empty!

My pocket was empty.

The internal cartwheels of success turned into body blows of embarrassment. My entire soul felt as if it withered and left my body. The emotional buzz of sealing the deal was quickly overturned by the gut-wrenching nausea that followed my realization.

What had I just done? Was I about to unwind this deal because of my negligence?

I began to play out every scenario in my head. I had no collateral… not even my driver's license, which was also in my wallet. After a brief journey to the restroom to contemplate my options and splash some cold water on my face, I was face-to-face with my client again for the moment of truth.

Asking my client to cover the bill was a humbling experience, one he joyfully reminded me of for years.

We'd present the invoice at the end of a project, and he'd ask me, "Who's paying?"

The humiliation from that day lingered, prompting a need for change.

Act 2: THE PERSEVERANCE

It was that embarrassing lunch that prompted a decision to make a change.

I realized the need for a systematic approach to avoid repeating such lapses. I couldn't keep doing the same thing and expecting a different result. As famed motivational coach, Tony Robbins says, *"Change happens when the pain of staying the same is greater than the pain of change."* From time to time, I would show up at the office missing one of the critical elements that kept me prepared to run my day effectively. Phone. Wallet. Belt. Watch. Keys.

The "Five Taps" hack was born, ensuring I never left essential items behind. This practice evolved into a set of ensuing hacks that became invaluable in various aspects of my life.

The "Five Taps" became a cornerstone of my routine, a moment of pause at the front door, tapping each crucial item—phone, wallet, belt, watch, keys.

And off I would go.

What began as a forced, conscious intention soon became a rote and ingrained practice, a valuable habit aiding my success.

How would I describe these hacks?

Mnemonic Devices.

What are mnemonic devices?

You've used a mnemonic device if you've ever used a rhyme or a song to help you memorize something. It's simply a fancy word for a memorization tool.

These mnemonic hacks can help you remember anything from phone numbers to long lists to other things that would be otherwise difficult to remember.

This ritual of using mnemonic hacks became a widespread practice in all aspects of my life. I began to name the hacks, using easy-to-remember acronyms and titles for each. They helped me remember people's names, presentation lines, physical fitness prompts, positive mindset quotes, and more.

Think back to grade school and some of the memorization techniques you may have used:

The ABC song for the 26-letter alphabet...

"I before E, except after C" as a spelling rule...

"Please Excuse My Dear Aunt Sally" for the order of math equations.

My family and friends would give me a hard time about the hacks, but they worked like magic for me.

In the years that followed, I would go on a personal development journey to look within; a lifelong pursuit of becoming the best version of myself.

Through this process, I had my "Eureka" moment, leaving the golden handcuffs of the corporate world and pursuing my *"ikigai"*; a Japanese concept referring to something that gives a person a sense of purpose, *"a reason for being"*.

In this next "act", I led a nonprofit organization building water wells in developing countries around the world. I hung up my business suit and briefcase for blue jeans and a backpack. I learned more about myself in those years than in all of my previous years combined.

During that time, I was often asked for input, insight, and advice for finding purpose in life. In other words, "How do I find the same joy you've found by following your heart?"

I found myself offering the lessons I had accumulated through years of experience, applying personal development, and stepping out of my comfort zone into foreign territory… literally and figuratively.

What I came to realize is that hacks founded on principles resulted in healthy habits… healthy habits lead to healthy actions… and healthy actions lead to positive results in ALL AREAS OF LIFE.

As I laid the groundwork for teaching these hacks and principles, a curriculum was formed and my coaching practice was born. This was a divine calling. My next "act".

Act 3: THE CHARACTER

What I learned about life through this set of experiences was that most people go through life on a roller coaster.

Most people go from 0 - 100% in one area of their life in reaction to an inciting event; the loss of a job, a major health diagnosis, a child suffering from mental health, a failing marriage, etc. They respond by focusing their attention on this area of life. They get back on track for a while until they're back in their comfort zone. The next life event happens taking them on another dip in the ride. They give that area attention until they get back in their comfort zone yet again. This pattern goes on and on throughout life until, one day, they look back and question what they accomplished on the journey… and then the journey is over. What's the through line? A flat line. I would define this flat line as a life lived in mediocrity. Boring. Average. Below life's god-given potential.

Most of us know we're born to do more… we just don't take the step beyond our comfort zone to grow; to reach our full potential.

So how do we grow most effectively?

You've heard countless authors and so-called authorities prescribe different tactics for overcoming life problems whether they be spiritual, mental, physical, relational, or financial.

We've all seen these listicles:

'5 ways to total wellbeing'

'10 hacks to end procrastination'

'7 mindset secrets to change your life today'

Let's face it, there are millions of these speedy and simple self-help pieces on the internet.

We read them… get excited about the possible result… write down a list of actions we're going to take… then, do nothing!

Of course, we're conditioned to look for a fast and easy solution to these challenges in this day and age. Why, because there's a shortcut to everything. Microwaves for food, 10-minute workouts for the perfect body, pharmaceutical drugs for any and every ailment, and Alexa for answering any random question we can dream up.

Without the tough work of understanding the foundation of these challenges, the quick fixes just won't work.

So, where do we gain understanding?

I recall a set of matching brown & white hard-bound books in my childhood home that practically cost my folks the price of their car. Yes, Encyclopedias. And, when we had a question about something (seeking **knowledge**), we were directed to that source. It required finding the book labeled with the letters about the topic we wanted to research (seeking **understanding**). Once we fully comprehend the subject, we can apply this knowledge in real-world situations.

Let's take, for example, the carburetor in the first vehicle I purchased; a 1985 Jeep.

"Carburetor". Alphabetically, that would be in the book labeled "Bo-Ce". Search for the topic. Read to understand how a carburetor provides the right mix of fuel and air together to send the mixture into the engine cylinders for ignition and powering the vehicle. Apply what I had just learned by getting under the hood and making calculated adjustments to the air and gas intake valves (seeking **wisdom**).

This is the same approach that Elon Musk used to develop SpaceX.

What's this approach? FIRST PRINCIPLES

First principles thinking is the act of boiling a process down to the fundamental parts that you know are true and building up from there.

In 2002, Musk began his quest to send the first rocket to Mars.

After researching aerospace manufacturers around the world, Musk determined the cost of purchasing a rocket was astronomical, so he began to rethink the problem.

"I tend to approach things from a physics framework," Musk said in an interview. *"Physics teaches you to reason from first principles rather than by analogy. So I said, okay, let's look at the first principles. What is a rocket made of? Aerospace-grade aluminum alloys, plus some titanium, copper, and carbon fiber. Then I asked, what is the value of those materials on the commodity market? It turned out that the materials cost of a rocket was around two percent of the typical price."*

Instead of buying a finished rocket for tens of millions, Musk decided to create his own company, purchase the raw materials for cheap, and build the rockets himself. SpaceX was born.

Within a few years, SpaceX had cut the price of launching a rocket by nearly 10x while still making a profit. Musk used first principles thinking to break the situation down to the fundamentals, bypass the high prices of the aerospace industry, and create a more effective solution.

I was only fixing my $4,000 Jeep... Elon was building $390M rockets.

Nevertheless, the approach was the same.

First Principles thinking requires 3 key ingredients:

Knowledge - information

Understanding - Comprehension

Wisdom - Application

By analyzing the challenges I was facing in life (along with the rest of humanity), I had landed on something...

I concluded that there are 5 fundamental problems with the vast majority of us seeking personal development... Let's use a listicle:

Desire for Fast Results: We want results fast, with a microwave mentality, unwilling to take the stairs to success.

Preference for Easy Solutions: We desire results without practice, lacking the discipline to build the necessary muscle for success.

Comparison to Others: We want results others have, driven by FOMO, and fail to channel inward growth.

One-Size-Fits-All Mentality: We believe it's a one-size-fits-all solution, disregarding our unique personality and character.

Backward Pursuit of Results: We want results backward, often starting with financial goals and ending with spiritual goals.

"It's not what you've got, it's what you use that makes a difference." —Zig Ziglar

Act 4: THE HOPE

The greatest Principle of all... **You Reap what you Sow**.

That's right... I've boiled down all of PERSONAL DEVELOPMENT to this basic truth... What you invest your time, talent, and treasure in will produce the fruit of that investment.

Good thoughts produce good fruit. Bad thoughts produce bad fruit.

But here's the catch... There is no One-Size-Fits-All approach. We're all built and bred differently. What works for my mental health may not work for the next person. What diet works for me may not work for the next person. What prescription works for me may not work for the next person. What morning routine works for me may not work for the next person. And so on.

Dr. Andrew Huberman, professor of neurobiology at Stanford, started a podcast to bring zero-cost information about our physiology to help us optimize sleep, exercise, nutrition, and more. Before giving practical takeaways, he would always explain the theory (principles) first. Understanding how the body works is key before applying tactics.

So, what solution am I offering here?

Know thyself.

That's right... start by knowing thyself. Knowing thyself is the most fundamental step in the First Principle for personal development.

If you don't understand how a tree is formed, how can you help it grow? If you don't know how a carburetor functions, how can you fix it? If you don't understand yourself, how can you live up to your potential and fulfill your purpose?

Knowing your God-given purpose will set the vision for your life and bring the greatest fulfillment.

This is a First Principles approach. Once you understand what you were designed to bring to this world, you can begin on the journey of practicing actions daily that move you closer to that purpose.

From there, you've got to set goals, establish a process, and develop discipline.

Goals are the desired states that people seek to obtain, maintain, or avoid. Think of them as a set of blocks that, when stacked upon each other, lead to a greater achievement. It's often said that going through life without goals is like a boat without a rudder... directionless and governed by the winds of fate.

Process is a series of actions or events performed to make something or achieve a particular result. Think of the process as the plan or ladder that gets you to the top of each of your goals.

Discipline is the highest form of self-love. It is delaying instant gratification and comfort for something greater in the future. It's living up to the promises we make to ourselves, consistently. It moves us from thinking to doing, to being. Discipline is what differentiates good from great.

"It sounds simple telling people to work hard and never quit, but to really execute and demonstrate those principles takes discipline and faith. Those are the two factors that I believe separate the good from the great, the successes from the failures." - Nipsey Hussle

True self-love is the hardest yet most rewarding thing you can ever do.

The formula is simple… but not easy.

It's only that very small select group of people, who take the time to dig deep within, understand their purpose, and manifest their potential, living the life that our creator designed for us, who reach a level of satisfaction that comes from transcendence.

Joe Dispenza poses this question, ***"Can you accept the notion that once you change your internal state, you don't need the external world to provide you with a reason to feel joy, gratitude, appreciation, or any other elevated emotion?"***

Our creator must think… "I've given each of my creations so much potential, yet so few make the effort to unlock it."

Call it lack of training, lack of desire, lack of understanding, cultural conditioning, or external validation.

Whatever the cause, the result is tragic.

It's time to break free from the habits that keep us in the sheep mentality; mindlessly going through life on someone else's terms. It's time to step out of our comfort zones to reach for more. It's time to take risks.

These all start by looking inward.

And, once we look inward, discover truths, change our mindset, and believe in our future; we begin to live elevated, extraordinary lives.

It's time to find purpose.

It's time to change.

"The greatest tragedy is not death, but life without purpose." - Dr. Myles Munroe

Romans 5:3-4 tells us, ***"We also glory in our sufferings because we know that suffering produces perseverance; perseverance, character; and character, hope."***

Through our challenges, we learn essential qualities that ultimately help us become prepared to live out our purpose.

In conclusion, the journey from suffering to hope is a comprehensive exploration of personal development. From the corporate climb to the character's evolution, the fundamental problems, and the unveiled hope, each act contributes to a holistic understanding of the principles that drive growth. It's a call to action, urging individuals to break free from mediocrity, embrace discipline, and live a life aligned with their purpose. As the journey unfolds, it becomes evident that personal development is not a one-size-fits-all solution but a personalized, intentional, and transformative path toward an extraordinary life.

My life mission is to become the greatest version of myself and to share that gift with the world.

I'm honored to be a coach leading people to wealthy lives spiritually, mentally, physically, relationally, and financially.

***

To contact Victor:

info@victorhailey.com

www.victorhailey.com

www.TheMoneyVictor.com

linkedin.com/in/victorhailey

IG: @victorhailey

IG: @TheMoneyVictor

Kathryn Brown

Kathryn Brown's entrepreneurial journey is rooted in the unwavering support of God. Her passion for health, wellness, leadership, and mindset stems from her own experience of overcoming trauma, where she found strength and guidance through her faith. Through her platform, "Take Back Your Health," Kathryn empowers individuals to reclaim their well-being through nutrition, leadership, and mindset coaching.

With a deep belief in the power of God, Kathryn illuminates the path for those seeking transformation. Her coaching approach extends beyond physical needs, incorporating compassion and spirituality to strengthen belief systems and cultivate resilience. By addressing the physical and mental aspects of well-being, Kathryn equips her clients with the tools and strategies necessary for enduring change.

Setting an example, Kathryn embodies her teachings, becoming a beacon of hope for those striving to thrive in all areas of life. Her unwavering faith and entrepreneurial spirit highlight the transformative power of embracing faith and taking inspired action.

The impact of Kathryn's coaching is evident in the lives she touches. Guided by God's unwavering support and her expertise, she helps individuals achieve optimal health and cultivate a resilient mindset. She reminds her clients that faith provides continuous support, even in the darkest moments, enabling positive transformation to take place.

Kathryn Brown's coaching, deeply rooted in her faith, serves as a catalyst for lasting change. Her journey and teachings exemplify the power of relying on God's support. With unwavering faith, individuals can overcome any obstacle and lead a transformed life.

Hope Road: From Struggles to Surrender, Finding Purpose in Empowering Others.

By: Kathryn Brown

From the very beginning, I was faced with the challenge of being adopted, which fueled a deep sense of abandonment and a constant search for love and belonging.

This book serves as a testament to surrendering to a higher power and embracing vulnerability to invite miracles into our lives. It showcases the transformative love and grace of God, revealing a divine plan beyond our comprehension. Through my personal journey of facing challenges and surrendering to divine guidance, I discovered the power of nutrition, personal development, and faith-based entrepreneurship. These experiences have not only transformed me but have fueled my passion to assist others on their wellness and empowerment journeys.

Throughout my life, I carried the burden of feeling unloved and unwanted. The fear that everyone would eventually leave me loomed over my head, creating a constant need for validation. Adversities such as experiencing sexual trauma and enduring abuse from many of the relationships in my life only exacerbated those feelings of worthlessness. However, amidst the darkness, I found solace in running.

At the tender age of twelve, I embarked on a significant journey by participating in my first 10k race in Montreal, Canada. Surpassing expectations, I achieved second place among women, a remarkable feat that ignited a glimmer of hope within me. Encouraged by my running coach, who saw great potential in me, he envisioned my path leading to the 1992 Olympics and began training me accordingly. However, as life would have it, unexpected circumstances took me on a different path.

Relocating from Ontario to British Columbia shattered the dreams I had woven around my future in running and becoming an Olympic athlete. Due to the lack of professional training I struggled to find motivation on my own as a teenager, I turned to unhealthy coping mechanisms, such as drinking, smoking, and seeking validation through unfulfilling, codependent, promiscuous relationships lacking emotional depth and authenticity. My life entered a perpetual cycle of placing others' needs before my own, constantly yearning for love and acceptance.

While my dreams of becoming an Olympic runner seemed to have disintegrated, a divine intervention was quietly at work. My father, unbeknownst to me, had been entering my name every time he visited a Petro Canada gas station to fill up for gas. As fate would have it, I was chosen to carry the Olympic torch for the 1988 Winter Olympics Torch Relay, a momentous opportunity embedded in God's overarching plan. It was a reminder that I was destined to be an Olympic runner, and my life could have taken a vastly different path.

Instead, I went on a path of destruction, becoming a party girl, attending raves, consuming explicit drugs and alcohol. Getting into relationships with men who were unavailable and saw me as an object. In 2008, after enduring yet another abusive relationship, I took a courageous step towards healing. I sought help from a psychologist and learned about Emotional Freedom Techniques (EFT) tapping. These therapeutic interventions became catalysts for personal growth. In 2012 I searched for spiritual enlightenment, I embarked on a profound week-long quest with shamans, attended yoga classes and turned to a community of seekers.

In 2017 my relationship with my fiancé abruptly ended, leaving me once again grappling with feelings of abandonment and heartbreak. To add to my emotional turmoil, a breast cancer scare in 2018 further challenged my resilience, as I faced medical complications during the biopsy procedure.

I was brought into the room and the medical staff proceeded to set up everything in front me, which brought terror to my heart, I was scared. It then took the staff over forty-five minutes to get me set up on the table, I was laying on my right side, arms and legs out. One of the staff members then said, we want you to hear the sound of the biopsy instrument, it sounded like a staple gun on steroids, fear set in. As I lay there, they asked that I remain completely still, they went in for the first biopsy and I started to cry not knowing if the freezing would work. I began to say in my head, be still, be still. In that moment the medical staff asked if I was on blood thinners, I said, no. I was bleeding out, due to the biopsy going through two of my veins. They went in nine times, taking out nine pieces of my breast, each the size of a grain of rice.

Growing up without a sense of trust in others, I faced additional hurdles within my professional life. For two decades, I dedicated myself to my job, yet suffered from bullying, harassment, and discrimination for thirteen of those years. Each day felt like an uphill battle, further eroding my already fragile trust in humanity.

In the year of 2020, my world was once again shattered when a shocking revelation came to light: I was conceived through rape. This painful truth sent me spiraling into a profound identity crisis and a deep sense of loss. As if that wasn't enough, later that same year, my employer forced me onto employment insurance, further exacerbating my feelings of losing a part of myself. By November, the weight of it all became unbearable, and I found myself on the brink of despair.

In the depths of my darkest moment, as despair threatened to consume me, I grappled with a nagging thought: What had I accomplished in my life? I was unmarried, without children, lacking a clear vision or purpose. I felt like a burden, worthless and insignificant. The memories of past abuses, the heartbreak of failed relationships, the fleeting pleasures that only left me feeling empty, and the torment of workplace bullying all collided, creating an overwhelming burden that seemed impossible to bear.

It was in this desperate hour that I thought about ending my life. It is also the moment that I turned to God, baring my soul and pouring out my deepest anguish. In a state of raw vulnerability, I begged for my life to end and in the same breath asked for divine guidance and intervention. In that moment of surrender, it was as though I could hear God say, "finally, she surrendered."

Since that pivotal moment, God has been leading me through an extraordinary metamorphosis. It has been a profound journey of self-discovery, reigniting hope, and shifting my perspective on the possibilities of life. With God as my guiding light, I have embarked on a path guided by His wisdom and love.

Through this transformative encounter with the Holy Spirit, I have come to understand that my worth and purpose are not defined by societal standards or past disappointments. I have discovered a renewed sense of self-worth and a deep appreciation for the beauty of life's journey. With each step forward, led by God's presence, I am finding my place within the intricate tapestry of creation.

Embarking on my journey to empower others on their wellness paths was far from a straightforward and predictable process. It was a winding road, characterized by personal challenges, moments of profound self-discovery, and undeniable guidance from God. I not only found healing for my own wounds, but I also discovered an innate desire to assist others in reclaiming their health and transforming their lives.

As the demands of my employer became increasingly unbearable between the years 2021 and 2022, I grappled with the devastating effects on my mental, physical, and spiritual well-being. This led to a period of necessary stress leave, during which I relied on welfare for financial support while I awaited the completion of paperwork. In those moments of immense challenges, a profound lack of purpose and direction consumed me.

Once again, I surrendered to God, taking it a step further by completely entrusting my life into His capable hands and earnestly seeking His divine guidance. It was within that deeper surrender that the path to healing and purpose began to slowly reveal itself. God's guiding hand led me to an extraordinary company called Purium, renowned for their commitment to providing high-quality superfoods and supporting individuals on their transformative journeys. Recognizing the urgent need for my own healing, I wholeheartedly embraced Purium's offerings, nurturing my body and rejuvenating my spirit.

Underpinned by divine direction, I embarked on a remarkable voyage of wellness that ignited my passion for personal development and inspired leadership. This profound calling led me to a life-changing program called HeartCore Leadership, immersing myself in a world of growth and self-discovery. Through this

The Change[20]

transformative program, I gained a newfound sense of clarity, embraced my unique strengths, and tapped into the boundless potential that resided within me.

During my leadership training, something truly remarkable happened on June 27, 2021. Surrounded by my family and church community, I was blessed with the opportunity to be baptized in the ocean where I live. As I stepped into the water, I felt a wave of emotions washing over me, and I knew deep in my heart that this was the moment when I would be cleansed and made new in Christ.

After the baptism, as I returned home and settled on my couch, I began reflecting on the events of the day. I marveled at the wonders of God and the divine presence that was so palpable in that sacred moment. I was filled with gratitude that my family had been able to witness this significant step in my spiritual journey.

Suddenly, as I prepared to rise from the couch, I felt an overwhelming pressure bearing down on me. It was as if an unseen force was pushing against me, threatening to crumble my legs beneath me. Puzzled and slightly alarmed, I uttered aloud, "What is happening?"

In that instant, I heard the unmistakable voice of God resonating deep within my being. His voice was clear and resolute as he spoke, "I want you to feel what you have been carrying all these years."

Confused yet open to His guidance, I responded, "What?" It was as if I needed further clarification to fully comprehend His words.

Once again, God spoke, affirming His purpose, "I want you to feel what you have been carrying all these years one last time."

As I absorbed His instruction, the weight upon me intensified. Every burden, every pain, every struggle that I had carried throughout my life seemed to converge upon me in that moment. It was a profound and transformative experience, as if an invisible hand was ensuring that I would truly understand the weight I had borne.

But then, just as suddenly as the pressure had descended upon me, God's touch shifted. It was as if His divine hands reached down and cradled me gently in His palms. In that instant, I felt a release, a lifting of the burdens that had accumulated over the years. I was bathed in a sense of profound peace and overwhelming love.

As I reflect on that extraordinary day, I am filled with gratitude for the experience. God allowed me to feel the weight I had carried until that point so that I could fully appreciate the transformation and liberation that comes from surrendering to Him. In His infinite grace, He washed away my past and lifted me up, a living testament to His power and love.

That day will forever remain etched in my heart as a reminder of God's faithfulness and His unwavering presence in my life. It was a tangible manifestation of His desire to free me from the burdens of the past and carry me forward into a new and purposeful life in His Name.

Fueled by my noteworthy progress, I not only successfully completed the program but also took an active role in staffing and mentorship in the trainings offering unwavering support to numerous individuals on their respective leadership journeys.

My work with Purium and HeartCore Leadership became the catalyst for my personal and professional transformation. I witnessed the profound impact that holistic wellness can have on individuals, not only in terms of physical health but also in terms of their overall well-being. It awakened within me an unyielding passion to guide others towards their own path of healing and self-discovery.

Growing through these experiences, I realized the power of community and connection in personal growth. I sought out and joined communities of like-minded entrepreneurs and leaders, who shared a common goal of creating positive change in the world. Through networking, collaboration, and shared wisdom, I found a supportive ecosystem that fueled my entrepreneurial aspirations while also prioritizing holistic health and wellness.

Today, I humbly stand as a faith-based entrepreneur, combining my passion for wellness, personal development, and spiritual alignment to guide and support others in reclaiming their health. I firmly believe that holistic well-being extends beyond physical health and includes mindset and spiritual vitality. Using my own journey as a catalyst, I provide coaching, mentoring, and actionable guidance to help individuals develop leadership skills, cultivate a positive mindset, and nourish themselves with optimal nutrition.

By integrating my faith and entrepreneurial spirit, I seek to create a ripple effect of positive change in the lives of those I serve. My purpose is to help individuals reclaim their health, transform their mindset, and embrace a lifestyle rooted in wellness and purpose. Through tailored programs, workshops, and one-on-one support, I empower individuals to tap into their full potential, rewrite their narratives, and lead fulfilling lives.

My mission is to guide thousands of people towards overall well-being through the pillars of leadership, mindset, and nutrition. I firmly believe that these elements are essential for healing past traumas, navigating difficult times, and refusing to be held back by life's challenges.

These three pillars work in synergy to empower us to overcome obstacles and live fulfilling lives. Leadership allows us to take responsibility for our health and make proactive choices. By assuming a leadership role in our own well-being, we can create healthy habits that support and nourish our bodies and minds. Developing a positive mindset is also crucial as it fosters resilience, enabling us to overcome adversity and transform from victims to victors in our own lives. Lastly, nutrition plays a vital role in fueling our bodies and providing the necessary nutrients for vibrant health.

Together, these elements create a powerful framework for reclaiming our health and embracing a fulfilling life.

1. Being in Responsibility and Empowerment:

At the heart of my approach lies the concept of being in responsibility for our own health. I firmly believe in empowering individuals to take charge of their health journey and make proactive choices that support their well-being. By embracing this mindset, individuals can cultivate a clear and powerful state of mind, enabling them to create healthy habits that nourish their bodies and souls.

2. Detoxification: Cleansing the Physical and Emotional Toxins:

Detoxification serves as a crucial pillar in my vision of reclaiming health. I advocate for releasing both physical and emotional toxins, recognizing the profound impact that unresolved emotions can have on our overall well-being. Physical detoxification involves supporting the body's natural cleansing processes through practices such as hydration, clean eating, and exercise. Emotional detoxification revolves around acknowledging and processing lingering traumas that may be holding individuals back from reaching their full potential. By purging the body and mind of toxic elements, individuals can optimize their functionality and work in harmony with their goals, rather than against them.

3. Mindful Eating and Nourishment:

Addressing cravings is an essential component of my approach. I recognize the significance of mindful eating and nourishing our bodies with nutrient-dense foods. This method involves cultivating a conscious awareness of our hunger and satiety signals, as well as fostering a positive relationship with food. By shifting our mindset around food, we can find satisfaction in making nourishing choices that provide sustained energy, mental clarity, and vibrant health. Mindful eating allows us to savor the joy of nourishing our bodies, while also honoring our unique dietary needs and preferences.

4. Restoring Gut Health:

I recognize the fundamental role that our gut plays in maintaining optimal health and advocate for resetting the body on a cellular level. Prioritizing gut health brings numerous benefits, including enhanced digestion, a stronger immune system, improved mental and emotional well-being, weight management support, improved nutrient absorption, reduced inflammation, glowing skin, and increased energy and vitality. Strategies for maintaining or improving gut health include consuming a diverse and balanced diet rich in fiber and fermented foods, staying hydrated, managing stress levels, engaging in regular exercise, avoiding excessive use of antibiotics, and incorporating probiotics and prebiotic-rich foods into our lifestyles.

5. Quality Sleep for Vitality:

Emphasizing the importance of quality sleep is another vital aspect of my approach. A good night's sleep serves as a crucial pillar of overall well-being, contributing to cognitive function, emotional well-being, and physical recovery. By addressing issues such as brain fog and promoting mental clarity through quality sleep, individuals can unlock their full potential and make the most of each new day. Creating a sleep routine that prioritizes restful sleep habits, such as maintaining a consistent sleep schedule, creating a soothing sleep environment, and engaging in relaxation techniques, can significantly enhance overall vitality and well-being.

Conclusion:

As I walk in faith, relentlessly pursuing my vision, my ultimate goal is to reach and empower thousands of individuals. Together, we can create an empowering movement to reclaim well-being, extending positive change to our communities. I firmly believe that healing is attainable for everyone, through the healing powers of the Holy Spirit. I am dedicated to supporting individuals on their unique journeys by integrating principles of leadership, mindset, and nutrition.

My vision for reclaiming health is centered around core principles that empower individuals to take responsibility for their well-being. Together, we can rewrite the prevailing narratives around health, leadership, and personal growth, ushering in an era of empowered and purpose-driven living.

***

To contact Kathryn:

Phone Number: 236-333-7291

Email: kathrynbrown@plantbasedhealer.com

Website: https://linktr.ee/Aliveintheword333

Social Media:

Facebook:

Personal Page: https://www.facebook.com/Kathryn1126?mibextid=LQQJ4d

Private Facebook Group:

https://m.facebook.com/groups/228536102298335/?ref=share&mibextid=S66gvF

LinkedIn: https://www.linkedin.com/in/kathryn-brown-1787621b9

Instagram: https://instagram.com/aliveintheword3?igshid=NGVhN2U2NjQ0Yg==

David Norris

David Norris is a husband, father, grandfather, leader, former banker, and served as an Infantry Officer in the United States Marine Corps.

Formerly, Happy State Bank's Chief Operating Officer, David's bank operations experience of 35 years covers the spectrum of bank operations, investments, asset-liability management, interest rate risk, enterprise risk management, balance sheet management, loan operations and administration, mortgage lending operations, information technology, corporate trust, wealth management, human resources, accounting, facilities management, regulatory compliance, and audit.

For 25 years, David helped Happy State Bank grow from a two-location company of $20 million in total assets to its 35 locations in 24 communities and nearly $3 billion in total assets and is now one of the largest banks in Texas. He has also been the team lead on eleven bank mergers and acquisitions.

An executive and entrepreneur leadership consultant and coach since 2015, David has dedicated his life to empowering, growing, and mentoring business owners, entrepreneurs, and CEOs to become better leaders because nothing in any enterprise improves until the leader improves.

David's education includes a Bachelor of Science from Texas A&M University and Master of Business Administration (MBA) from Chapman University.

Is it Good to be You?

By David Norris

I have been saying that it is good to be me for some time. The truth is that it is good to be me. I am very good at being me. Nobody in the world is as good as I am at being me. I get to do lots of things. I go places, meet wonderful people, and have the most amazing friends and relationships. These relationships span the globe and for one reason alone……I choose it.

And while it has always been good to be me, I didn't always recognize how good it was to be me. I was victim to the mental games of comparison and validation and along with many other paradigms and ways of thinking to which we subject ourselves. Never good enough…Try harder…Good things come to those who wait…Better safe than sorry…Look before you leap…Don't do that…What will the neighbors think?…Who do you think you are?...Money doesn't grow on trees.

It wasn't until I chose to overcome being average or being mediocre and instead choose to live a life that is abundant, noteworthy, successful, and significant that I began to see how good it was to be me. It all started with making a decision… a decision that I AM worthy and deserving to have the life and lifestyle I want and deserve.

Perhaps my story is like yours. I decided on a career path to follow as I prepared for my future after graduation from college. A career plan that had me thinking this was the answer to my eventual success personally and economically. First, I learned the skills required to be the best Marine officer I could be whether that was putting steel on the target or loading a battalion of men and equipment on ships to travel across the Pacific Ocean. I expanded this skillset learned in the Marine Corps when I began my career in banking. My early lessons in leadership translated to expanding the skillset of lenders, operations and front-line people to make my organization the best in its market. Doing the skills of banking better than the other guy in a largely commoditized industry is essential to the growth and prosperity and longevity within the organization. What I didn't realize was this was only one dimension to a greater path every individual must engage in if they truly want to live a life of abundance. A life of abundance is what everyone should strive to accomplish. In accomplishing abundance, you will live a life that is noteworthy, successful and significant. Abundance is much more than a monetary goal. It includes health and wellness, relationships, vocation, and time and money-freedom. To live an abundant life you must follow a personal growth plan. A personal growth plan is a mindset transformation to a mindset of abundance.

The development of a different mindset is not a new idea. In the 1800's people such as Ralph Waldo Emerson, Henry David Thoreau, and Louisa May Alcott would sit around a table and discuss a life unimagined by many. The basis was changing their mindset. Time and time again we see companies fail or fade away while others grow and prosper. Companies and organizations that prosper have the best leadership at all levels. They consistently maintain their relevance in the marketplace and consistently produce, grow, and develop their people. This is because companies not only work on the business aspects of their organization but also the mindset. These companies understand that if their employees do not have the right mindset both individually and corporately, they will not achieve abundance. The Bible says we are not to be conformed to this world but be transformed by the changing of our minds.

I can pinpoint the day my world was transformed. It was July 25, 1995 when my CEO gave me a book titled <u>Developing The Leader Within You</u> by John C. Maxwell. We devoted one officers meeting per month to studying a chapter. In 2000, I was elected president of my Rotary Club and was introduced to another John Maxwell book, <u>The 21 Irrefutable Laws of Leadership</u>. At this stage in my personal growth, I was awakened by Law #2 The Law of Influence. The Law of Influence states "Leadership is influence, nothing more, nothing less and everything rises and falls on leadership." In that chapter Dr. Maxwell writes about CEOs who ask him what they can do to determine the leadership potential or ability of their employees. Maxwell tells them to get them involved in leading volunteers. When you lead volunteers, you only have your ability to influence others going for you. There is no paycheck to dangle over their head, nothing but you and your own influence to see that a volunteer organization's goals and objectives are met.

The idea of influence so inspired me that I made the conscious decision to be the absolute best Rotary Club President that my Rotary Club had ever had. I had been in Rotary 17 years going through the motions of doing the Rotary thing without ever being a Rotarian. Having started on a path of personal growth, I no longer chose to follow just what was required but to step up and ask "this and what more is required to flourish?"

I attended President Elect Training, and my eyes were opened to the deeper meaning of Rotary. I heard many great and inspiring speakers and met the incoming President of Rotary International. I found this organization was truly making a positive impact on this world and that had a positive impact on me. More importantly, I met some fellow Presidents Elect that were very dynamic and giving people. A couple of them were single moms, raising a family on their own, giving back to their community. They were big time givers to The Rotary Foundation. The Rotary Foundation provides funds to fight disease, hunger, and suffering worldwide. I had participated in many Rotary Foundation fundraisers but never had I made a contribution outside the fundraising events. How were they able to do this? I was embarrassed and ashamed of myself and took action. I could do better.

At the end of the year, I was named the District's Rotary Club President of the Year. My club membership grew. Thirteen members, including me, donated $1,000 each to The Rotary Foundation. What makes this more important to my story is that this was the second time I had been selected to serve as president of a Rotary Club. I served my first Rotary Club as president 14 years earlier. I attended President Elect Training then and heard many of the same things. The difference was the lens through which I viewed my relationship to the world around me. I now viewed it through the lens of my personal growth plan. My mindset had changed to one that taught me that we are put on this planet to make a difference.

In 1991 I began work at Happy State Bank. I was in charge of bank operations. The bank was under new ownership and at the time, out of 880 banks in Texas, Happy State Bank was #812 with just over

$20 million in assets and two locations. Today, Texas has over 650 banks. Happy State Bank ranks at #27 at this writing. We have 34 locations in 24 different communities and over $2.5 billion in total assets.

We grew slowly at first, planted a few new branches in nearby towns in the Texas Panhandle and in 2004 embarked on the first of nine mergers and acquisitions. The CEO "hunted them down". My job was to "kill 'em, clean 'em, and cook 'em." That is, I was tasked with leading the team making the data processing conversion, mentoring the employees of the new bank to operate as a Happy Bank and assimilating the new employees into our culture. I was tasked in leading a corporate mindset change.

It was 2009 and Happy State Bank had just crossed the $1 billion in total asset mark when I was asked to serve as a Rotary District Governor. As a governor, you are one of 530 people in the world of 1.2 million Rotarians. It is a daunting task involving two years preparation and one year of actual service with a lot of travel. Most people simply will not do this at all and doing it while fully employed is considered insane. I was insane. The challenge here is that during that three-year process of becoming district governor, Happy State Bank would grow another $1 billion to $2 billion and complete four acquisitions. This tasked my leadership, our people and infrastructure.

I did not know how my new role as Governor was going to mesh with my work at Happy State Bank. I did know my bank culturally and historically and knew growth and expansion was in our DNA. I also knew I had a great team of leaders at Happy State Bank and Rotary that were there to support me. I felt there was high probability it could happen by choosing to allow my mindset to expand further to accomplish the tasks. I succeeded. During the busiest part of my tenure of District Governor, in March of 2012, I was promoted to Chief Operating Officer of Happy State Bank.

So what is the point, the matter, the issue, to this rambling? The point is most people accept what life gives them and settle for an average or mediocre life and simply will not step up to live the life they imagine because they are not aware they can. There is no quick fix to experience personal growth. It is an ongoing process of learning to accept your potential for greatness.

I have said several times that I chose to raise the level of my awareness as to my own leadership ability and potential. It would have been considerably easier to quit Rotary, or wait until I retired, or had more time, or not do it at all. Rather, I chose to step up and step into a life of my choosing. I chose to advance my life rather than retreat from it. This is what a personal growth plan is all about. Great and amazing things can happen when you consciously choose to expand your mindset and decide to raise your own potential.

During my post military career, I did what so many of us do and continue to do, to work, slave, and grind it out daily seeking to better our lives and the lives of our families, willing to accept whatever conditions and circumstance come our way, and glad to have a job. Undoing and unwinding decades of paradigms and bad habits takes time and gut-wrenching mental work. I did not do it by myself. I did not have the ability to do it myself. All I knew was I wanted to grow. I wanted something better. Having coaches and mentors to show me the way was necessary.

Yes, I read a few books. These books were the catalyst; however, what really happened is that I made a conscious decision to develop my plan of personal growth and take charge of my own personal development and live the life I chose to live. I chose to grow as a man and as a human being and not be a human pinball with everybody in the world having their own flipper.

I associated myself with some of the greatest minds in the world. I sought to study with and be coached and mentored by them. These great minds include my friend Paul Martinelli, Les Brown, John Maxwell, and my coach and mentor, Mary Morrissey. It is through their expert guidance and my decision to invest in myself that I accomplish the things that I say I want in life.

I placed myself in a position of permanent discomfort. So many people, when confronted with the discomfort of their own personal growth and development run back to their comfort zone. Attempts or efforts to grow are met with fear and they allow themselves to be pulled back into the herd by people close to them because average people have a vested interest in keeping you just like them.

The biggest thing my coaches and mentors taught me is to be grateful. Gratitude is the most important lesson because without it there is no growth. Without gratitude I am unable to receive any of the many blessings and grace God has given me and shown me.

- I am so grateful for my wife, Candy, and daughter Andi, and my entire family, especially my granddaughters.
- I am so happy and grateful for the United State Marine Corps and the opportunity to serve this Country and grow as a leader and as a man.
- I am so happy and grateful for Happy State Bank and the opportunity to work in a place with people who share the same core values, where growth is modeled and expected, and who encouraged me to pursue my endeavors in Rotary.
- I am so happy and grateful for Rotary for the opportunities to serve and make a difference in the lives of others, in particular fighting hunger right here in America and traveling to India to help rid that country of Polio.
- I am continuously grateful for everything including bank examiners, crabby customers, pushy arrogant people, and poor leaders because they helped me grow.

You see, I am on a mission and that mission is to be the absolute best version of myself so that I can make the world the absolute best version of itself. Athletes, top business executives, and entrepreneurs don't get to the top of their games without training plans and coaches to help them be just that, the best version of themselves regardless of their conditions and circumstances. So many people say, "I don't have the money" or "I don't have the time" or "I have to work". Those are conditions and circumstances used as excuses to not take action and remain stuck.

A person that really wants to grow, and truly wants to improve his or her life by creating an abundant life for him or herself will make the conscious decision to grow and develop themselves. They will do what they can, where they are, with what they have to reach their goal or dream. You are your most important asset. If you do not invest in yourself, why should anyone else?

Personal growth and development only requires a commitment to oneself. It does not require a person to quit a job or wait until a better job or environment or business comes along. Personal growth does not require waiting until the kids graduate or until you retire at some predetermined age or waiting until the economy improves. It only requires that you act now, in the present, wherever you are and doing what you can with what you have….and be continuously and constantly grateful.

Personal development and growth take intentional commitment to this work and staying connected to this work. If you really want to grow, if you really want to prepare yourself for that promotion to the C-Level suite, if you really want to start your own business, build that dream home, or find that soulmate, start where you are, do what you can with what you have AND get a coach or an accountability partner. Engage in studies and mastermind groups to help you navigate your journey.

Do what I did or find what works for you. Just make some room for yourself. Be responsible and accountable to yourself for creating new space for new opportunities. Stop watching television and read a book instead. Unsubscribe from that daily digital distraction known as email and take action to stop them rather than letting them accumulate. Listen to audio books in the car rather than the radio.

There is opportunity for personal development everywhere if you just create room for it and exploit the opportunity when it comes. The opportunity is already there for you so have the courage to dream big about the life you would love to live. Take an action step every day even if it is a baby step and at the very least believe that I believe you can do this. You will soon discover that it can be as good to be you as it is good to be me.

***

Learn more about David Norris and his work at:

https://www.linkedin.com/in/superdavenorris

Contact David Norris at:

806-679-9326

david@davidnorrisleadership.com

Erin Birch

Erin Birch is a soul having a human experience just like you! She is a mom of 2 grown boys, Wyatt and Jack, and lives on Vancouver Island on the west coast of Canada. The great outdoors and travelling are 2 of Erin's passions.

Erin is a personal transformation coach helping people rewire their minds and upgrade their identities by getting rid of past trauma and limiting beliefs and completely changing how they see themselves so that they can live a more joyous and fulfilling life!

Erin believes we can all BE, DO and HAVE anything we want in life, we just have to BECOME the person for which that can happen and become the person who can attract, manifest and create all the prosperity and abundance that we desire!

Erin is certified in several integrative techniques and strategies such as Neuro Linguistic Programming, Hypnosis, Emotional Release, Trama Release, Energy work and more, to help people create lasting change.

Erin is also a business coach who works with entrepreneurs building a business online using social media. Erin built a very successful business in a short amount of time and is passionate about helping others do the same.

A Midlife Crisis or a Midlife Awakening and Transformation

By Erin Birch

The Realization

I woke up on my 44th birthday and did the math! I thought, "Oh my God, I'm middle-aged"! "My life is half-lived, half over"! If I was going to live to the age of 88, then my life was indeed half over.

Was I depressed? No, I was shocked! How did this happen? I was 23 years old just yesterday!

As most of us do when we have this realization, I asked myself a few questions.

Am I happy? Am I fulfilled? Am I where I thought I would be at this point in my life? Is there enough excitement and passion in my life? Am I having enough fun and adventure? My bucket list! Am I checking things off?

Who am I? And why am I here? Am I living my purpose? What is my purpose, anyway?

I realized I wanted more out of life. I was feeling... stagnant.

I also realized that my happiness and fulfillment were up to ME, not anyone else! It was no one's job but my own. And I asked myself, "if not now, then when"?

If I don't make changes in my life now, then when? Because I wasn't getting any younger. My boys were teenagers and would be off on their own in a few years. What did I want the next chapter of my life to be like?

The Awakening

Midlife! A time of profound introspection!

You may be thinking, "Oh, she had a midlife crisis!" But I say I had a midlife realization–a realization that led to an awakening and a personal transformation!

It was a gift and a blessing!

So, what the heck IS a midlife crisis? The term was coined by Elliot Jacques, a Canadian psychoanalyst and social scientist, in the early 1960s. It is described as a psychological crisis brought about by events that cause a person to realize they are growing older, inevitable mortality, and possible lack of accomplishments. This CAN produce feelings of depression, remorse, and high levels of anxiety, or the desire to hold on to their youth, make drastic changes to their current lifestyle, or feel the wish to change past decisions and events.

Facing our own mortality! I had also just become aware of the book by Bronnie Ware called Regrets Of The Dying. Bronnie Ware was a palliative care nurse in Australia. She was at the bedside of patients who were dying. She couldn't help but notice that she was repeatedly hearing the same regrets from the dying.

These regrets were as follows:

1. I wish I had the courage to live a life true to myself not what was expected of me.
2. I wish I hadn't worked so hard.
3. I had the courage to express my feelings.
4. I wish I had stayed in touch with my friends.
5. I wish I had let myself be happier.
6. I wish I had cared less about what others think.
7. I wish I didn't worry so much.
8. I wish I hadn't taken life for granted.
9. I wish I had taken better care of myself.
10. I wish I had lived in the now.

This book had a significant impact on me! It was a gift of seeing what I, too, might regret and having time to do something about it! I had an AWAKENING! A big one! And I will be forever grateful for it because I am happier now than I have ever been. By the way, no one lays on their deathbed saying, I wish I had kept a cleaner house! Or, I wish I had made more money!

In my opinion, what makes it a crisis is how one deals with this realization!

What makes it a crisis is when you look OUTSIDE yourself for happiness and fulfillment. Some split up their marriage and look for a 23-year-old boyfriend or girlfriend, buy a sports car, maybe get into drugs and alcohol, and look for fulfillment outside themselves. Many people feel LOST during this stage of their life. People either look for fulfillment OUTSIDE themselves or realize happiness and fulfillment comes from within. This is what happened to me! I knew I would soon be an empty nester, so what did I want the next chapter of my life to be like?

In a very short period, I made many changes in my life. I had wanted to make many changes for years but needed more courage due to my limiting beliefs! I decided, if not now, then when? I shut down my business as an artisan Jeweler that I had been building for 17 years and started an all-online business that would be location-friendly and allow me to travel as I had always dreamed of being able to do. I loved designing and making jewelry but was tired of being the typical starving artist.

I went into marketing and struggled like crazy for my first four years as I had ZERO marketing or computer skills. I didn't even know how to copy and paste when I started my new business! I then realized not only was I lacking in the skills, but I was also lacking in the mindset needed to succeed. I knew I had to BECOME the person who could be successful.

I knew my identity and self-image would ultimately hold me back if I did not upgrade it.

I jumped into the world of personal development and fell in love with it. I became obsessed with it and traveled to many exotic locations to learn spirituality, meditation, quantum physics, neuro linguistic programming, hypnosis, energy healing, consciousness, and so many other things!!!

Even as a young child, I was always fascinated with the human mind, nature, and behavior. I remember when I was in grade four, and the class had to do a report. Most kids reported on dogs or cats. I did my report on cults. Yup, cults! I was fascinated by what made humans do what they did, what made them tick, and how people could be brainwashed. I thought I would go into psychology or criminology after high school, but my desire to travel and live abroad, at least for a few years, won out. So I moved to France! I returned from France, got into a relationship, married, and had kids.

Back to post-midlife realization and awakening…

I got into marketing and learned the craft. I had a very successful business within my first year. I then began to have people reach out to me and ask me to teach them how I had built my business and done it so fast. Voila, I found myself coaching. I also completely rewired my mind with all my personal work and became incredibly passionate about helping others do the same! Rewire their minds and become the person they wanted or were meant to be! I believe we are all much more capable than we think, and it is never too late to reinvent ourselves. Re-evaluate what you value most, what is most important to you. Our self-concept, how we see ourselves, and IDENTITY keep us believing nonsense about ourselves that keeps us playing small.

We tend to believe the limiting beliefs that we are not good enough, smart enough, pretty enough, thin enough, whatever enough, is the truth! Intellectually, we may know it is not true, but hell, the belief has been imprinted into our minds since childhood. We end up suffering from shallow confidence and low self-esteem, and our identity, how we see ourselves, becomes a self-fulfilling prophecy. Yikes! What you say to yourself about yourself becomes who you are.

I believed I was stupid and that I had a very low IQ. I believed it so completely that I came across as someone with a low IQ. I kept quiet in case someone figured it out, so people assumed I was. I played small in my life because I didn't believe I could play bigger and be successful. I didn't think I had what it took. Have you ever felt that way?

The beauty is that it does not have to take years and years of traditional therapy to get rid of the old story you keep telling yourself and create a new one! To get rid of those limiting beliefs holding you back! Who's got time for that? You have too much living to do! Most people dream of living their purpose and creating a ton of impact while they are here, leaving the world a better place! However, if we never upgrade our identity and have enough confidence and self-esteem to create that impact, then we don't.

It's never too late to change the way you see yourself! To go after what you want! Do you have a passion or a purpose you want to pursue or fulfill? And if you don't, that's ok too! Maybe your purpose is to be conscious, joyful, and help raise the planet's vibration. That in itself is no small purpose.

It's never too late to what I call UPGRADE YOUR IDENTITY! Discover who you truly are and what you truly value. Start being your authentic self and living with authenticity! Did you know that the frequency of authenticity is 4,000 times more powerful than love? And love is nothing to shake a stick at!

In life, we don't get what we want; we get who and what we are! We attract what we are a vibrational match to! What we are in alignment with! Being strong in your identity and being your authentic self-causes you to live at a higher vibration and frequency, which means you attract things, events, opportunities, and people of a higher vibration and frequency! And, when you are being authentic, you stop caring so much about what others think! How much happier would you be if you did not care what others thought? Nobody to bring down your vibe.

When living authentically, you are secure in who you are; you have higher confidence, self-esteem, and more trust and faith in yourself: less doubt and less fear. You are willing to take more calculated risks! Take more action in your business, career, and life! Maybe even approach that person that you've wanted to.

Another key to a successful and happy life besides upgrading your identity is something I work very hard on with my clients. And that is becoming very good at CONNECTING, being able to get into rapport with your fellow human beings and create a deep connection! This, of course, helps you thrive in business or your career and experience beautiful, strong, and meaningful relationships in your personal life!

I'm afraid that the art of connection is becoming lost with all this fandangled technology, and we can't allow that to happen. It's what makes us human. Yes, the art of connection and communication. How many relationships split up due to a lack of connection and communication? It's what the world needs: self-aware, compassionate, and empathetic souls who want to create deep connections with others.

One key to compassion is understanding that everyone has their map of reality! Your map of reality is different from mine and different from your neighbors. Knowing this makes us a lot more empathetic, compassionate, and less judgmental. It's tough to take things personally when you understand this—less hurt feelings. The meaning someone else gives something is due to their filter caused by past experiences, events, and beliefs. Often, how someone reacts has very little to do with us but with themselves. Projection is just human nature.

One of the most valuable things I have learned to do for myself and help my clients do for themselves is no matter what happens, be it an event, good, bad, or neutral, or an interaction with someone, I ask myself why I co-created it to happen! What am I meant to get from it or learn from it? How can I use it to become more self-aware and grow from it? This allows you to deal with things much more calmly and speeds up your personal growth. You almost look at things from a third-person point of view. It's a change of perspective that makes you less emotionally attached and less reactionary. It most certainly creates a more peaceful life!

When you know your values and live them, that is the secret to higher self-confidence and self-esteem. You become a person who knows what you want and goes after it! When you live your values, you have all the motivation you need, as motivation, too, comes from within. You can create a more peaceful, fulfilling life with all the prosperity and abundance you desire! You attract, and you manifest!

Being introduced to this world of personal development has been a lot of work but so worth it!

I am NOT the same person I used to be!

Would you agree it's worth it?

Because, after all, you don't want to have any regrets, do you?

***

To contact Erin:

www.erinbirchcoaching.com

Email erin@erinbirchcoaching.com

Facebook https://www.facebook.com/erin.birch.165

Sir James Gray Robinson, Esq.

Sir James Gray Robinson, Esq. is a third-generation trial attorney who specialized in family law and civil litigation for 27 years in his native North Carolina. Burned out, he quit in 2004 and has spent the next 20 years doing extensive research and innovative training to help others facing burnout and personal crises to heal. He has taught wellness, transformation, and mindfulness internationally to thousands of private clients, businesses, and associations. He is a licensed attorney focused on helping lawyers, professionals, entrepreneurs, employers, and parents facing stress, anxiety, addiction, depression, exhaustion, and burnout. He is a highly respected speaker, writer, TV personality, mentor, consultant, mastermind, and spiritual leader who is committed to healing the planet. He has over 30 certifications and degrees in law, healing, and coaching as well as hundreds of hours of post certification training in the fields of neuroscience, neurobiology and neuroplasticity, epigenetics, mind-body-spirit medicine, and brain/heart integration. He often speaks to professional associations about stress and burn out and has written over 9 books on personal growth and healing. In recognition of his work and philanthropy, he was knighted by the Royal Order of Constantine the Great and Saint Helen.

Changing Reality

By Sir James Gray Robinson, Esq.

Many people do not know that reality is subjective. They believe that whatever they perceive in their world is the one true "reality." Neuroscience has shown that this is not the case, and what we believe changes our perception of reality. For centuries humanity believed that our brains were unchangeable, and reality was fixed. We now understand that reality is fluid and is perceived differently from person to person.

Advances in our understanding of neuroplasticity have shown that our brain is malleable, and neuropathways change based on our thoughts, emotions, and beliefs. It was believed that we only used a small part of our brain for centuries, but we now understand that our entire brain is constantly active, but depending on the area of the brain that is activated we may or may not be aware of it..

The personal growth industry focuses on improving our physical, mental, emotional, spiritual, and financial lives. The most important component of personal growth is controlling our thoughts, emotions, beliefs, and behavior. Ever since Napoleon Hill wrote *"Think and Grow Rich"* in 1937, people have been striving to change their lot in life for the better by changing the way they think and behave.

When we better understand how our brains work, our ability to change our thoughts, behavior, and results becomes much more accessible and effortless. The science of Neuro Linguistic Programming (NLP) is focused on determining what thoughts and beliefs are causing the results in our life that we want to change and then changing those thoughts and ideas.

When we understand how the brain works, it is much easier to accomplish whatever result people want to achieve. Any coaching program that goes against fundamental brain function principles will not be successful, no matter how good the marketing program built around it. It would be like the weight loss industry, which makes billions of dollars a year selling products that are mainly placebos and have no effect on weight loss.

The brain makes up only 2 percent of our body weight, but it consumes 20 percent of the oxygen we breathe and 20 percent of the energy we consume. This enormous consumption of oxygen and energy fuels thousands of chemical reactions in the brain every second. These chemical reactions underlie our actions and behaviors to respond to our environment. In short, the brain dictates the behaviors that allow us to survive. More importantly, the brain dictates the behaviors that enable us to thrive.

The peripheral nervous system (PNS) directs sensory input from our five senses and skin to the central nervous system. The PNS comprises all nerve tissue outside the brain and spinal cord. The PNS delivers information from the body to the central nervous system. It is divided into two subsections: the sensory/somatic nervous system and the autonomic nervous system.

The somatic nervous system carries messages between the CNS and the body's sensory organs and voluntary muscles. It allows us to detect changes in the world around us and delivers information related to actions we decide to perform. This is our conscious behavior driven by our thoughts. In contrast, the autonomic nervous system carries messages between the CNS and our internal organs, as well as how we react to our environment. This is done unconsciously, instinctively and as a reaction to sensory input from our environment.

Our brain continuously processes signals through our eyes, ears, nose, mouth, and skin. In addition to the traditional five senses, scientists now recognize other sensations, including pain, pressure, temperature, joint position, and movement. These signals are processed through the autonomic nervous system first and then sent to the frontal cortex, which may take a few seconds to analyze sensory data. In other words, there is a gap between when we sense something and when we think about it. It is this gap that determines our reality.

Neurobiologists initially believed that the human brain was made of three distinct parts, from oldest to newest: (1) brain stem (fight or flight), (2) Limbic brain (emotions), and (3) Cortex (reasoning). It is now believed that these three parts are not independent but are collaborative, on a continuum between unconscious and conscious behavior.

We are now beginning to understand the role of neuroplasticity in our neurobiology. In the past, we believed that neural pathways were set and didn't change. Now, we understand that neuroplasticity allows new neural pathways to form as we learn further information and desire different results. When we change our thoughts and beliefs, we create new neural pathways. When we change our neural pathways, we change our thoughts and beliefs.

Our thoughts determine our neural pathways, and our neural pathways determine our thoughts, emotions, and behavior. Our neural pathways change as we learn new information or release negative thoughts, emotions, and behavior. You really can teach an old dog new tricks, or precisely, we can change how an old dog thinks.

The most recent neurological research has focused on our nervous systems. These nervous systems regulate how the rest of the brain interprets information. Nervous systems operate pre-thought and influence our behavior depending on how we perceive our environment. Our thoughts, emotions, and beliefs can alter how we perceive the environment, and our environment can change our thoughts, feelings, and beliefs.

The brain's most crucial function is to analyze our environment for safety or threat, predict our most optimum future and plan how to accomplish the future. We rely on memory, motivation, and cognitive beliefs to succeed or fail in our desired accomplishments.

Modern research has found that trauma can negatively impact our reasoning and perception skills. The pain and suffering from physical, emotional, or mental abuse can damage our hippocampus and amygdala, so that we experience maladaptive stress responses and chronic stress, depression, and anxiety.

For people that experience chronic stress, anxiety, or depression, the path to mental and emotional health can be fraught with walls and stumbling blocks. It is critical for people struggling with negative thoughts, emotions, and beliefs to identify the trauma that caused those symptoms and heal them. To change stumbling blocks into steppingstones, we must fearlessly accept our past and understand how it damages our future.

The oldest part of our brain on the evolutionary scale is the medulla and brainstem, which was the first organized brain after the original simple neural cells which controlled multicell organisms. This part of the modern brain is known as the reptilian brain and is millions of years old. This is where the autonomic nervous system is housed, which controls the body's automatic functions, such as breathing, digestion, heart rate, enzymes, and hormones.

The next part of the brain that evolved was the limbic brain, which consists of the amygdala, the hippocampus, and the thalamus. This part of the brain handles emotion, judgment, memory, and the production of various brain chemicals, such as melatonin, serotonin, and endorphins.

The latest evolution of the brain was the addition of the neocortex, or frontal cortex, which handles intellectual and executive function, language, communication, connection, rational thought, and civilization-building skills.

When we are stimulated through the five senses, this information is delivered first to the reptilian brain and then distributed through the limbic brain and neocortex for processing. The most important function of the reptilian brain is to classify information as safe or dangerous. It is important to remember that all of this occurs before the neocortex conscious parts receive it.

Life can be exhilarating or threatening—depending on how you view it. Millions of years ago, when our ancestors climbed out of the primordial ooze as reptiles, our brains looked far different than they do today. Hardly more than a cluster of cells with impulses and motor control, our brains didn't have the ability to think. They only reacted to threats in the environment. This was the beginning of our autonomic nervous system.

As indicated, the reptilian brain houses the autonomic nervous system. This system is divided into two parts, the sympathetic nervous system and the parasympathetic nervous system. The sympathetic nervous system is activated when the stimuli are perceived as a threat, while the parasympathetic nervous system is activated when the stimuli are perceived as safe.

I refer to the sympathetic nervous system as the Warrior and the parasympathetic nervous system as the Guru. This is because when the Warrior is activated, the brain and body react in fight or flight, while if the Guru is activated, the brain and body react as relax and digest. There is a sliding scale because both the Warrior and the Guru are always ready to engage and can activate simultaneously. However, certain bodily functions will occur depending on the Warrior being fully engaged, and vice versa,

This does not have anything to do with the conscious mind. We can't stop one or the other (Warrior or Guru) from activating. However, we can regulate one or the other with our conscious mind depending on whether we are aware of what is happening.

For example, many people get upset by the behavior of others that their autonomic nervous system interprets as threatening. Loud noises, inappropriate language, or injury can activate the Warrior. Threats, challenges, risky behavior (either inside or outside the body), and pain can activate the Warrior. My experience is that individuals in stressful jobs or unpleasant circumstances regularly activate their Warrior nervous system and rarely turn it off.

When the Warrior is activated, it signals the Limbic brain to go into defensive mode depending on the severity of the threat. We experience negative emotions such as anger, fear, rage, guilt, and remorse. The brain signals the body to produce adrenalin and cortisol, which signals the conscious brain to fight or flee. We can freeze, faint, or lose consciousness if the danger is severely dangerous. This is why some people will pass out if they are "scared to death."

The reasoning parts of the brain can shut down because the Warrior marshals all the body's resources for defense. Any energy not needed for fight or flight is diverted to the muscles. The digestive tract shuts down, and the heart rate and blood pressure increase, all due to evolution and survival of the fittest. However, it was only intended to be used temporarily until the danger passed.

Conversely, when we feel safe, and the Guru is activated, the brain produces melatonin, serotonin, and endorphins and signals the intestines to produce oxytocin. All these chemicals make us feel pleasant and relaxed. Our higher brain functions of reasoning and imagination come online, and we can love, be compassionate, converse, create, and cooperate. All of this is impossible when the Warrior is activated.

What we perceive depends on whether the Warrior or the Guru is activated. If an individual is not paying attention, they may not know which one is running the show. The problem is that people who live with the Warrior for any length of time have a far more negative perception of their environment because they focus on danger everywhere.

The ego originally evolved to assess and strategize fear and danger. Individuals who stay in their Warrior mode can experience high levels of stress and toxicity to their bodies because those are the natural results of the Warrior mode. It is the cause of burnout.

When operating with the Guru, life is fun, multidimensional, and safe. Thus, life is hard and dangerous when we are stuck with the Warrior. With the Guru, it is pleasant and easy. All of this is completely flying under the conscious spectrum of thought. When we say we create our reality, this is what is meant.

Today, we face many different threats than our ancestors. Instead of velociraptors, we must face unexpected negative results, adverse decisions, unhappy clients, rude adversaries, unexpected surprises, disappointments, and so on. The threats we face may not be life-threatening, but they may feel just as scary.

Without training, our autonomic nervous system reacts to threats, whether it is life-threatening or simply unexpected. Our sympathetic nervous system clicks on whenever it perceives a threat or simply is accustomed to activating. If we keep the Warrior activated continuously by thinking and rethinking about dangers or adverse events due to neuroplasticity, it becomes normalized, and we get used to it.

If we get used to an activated sympathetic nervous system, it feels uncomfortable when it turns off, and the threat is over. Then we may subconsciously create reasons to reactivate the system. In other words, we subconsciously create chaos to activate our sympathetic nervous system.

There are symptoms of an overactive Warrior in our psyche. These include:

- Anger
- Anxiety
- Insomnia
- Muscle pain and stiffness
- High blood pressure
- Weight gain
- Depression
- Compromised immune system.

It is no coincidence that many highly stressed individuals complain of these symptoms. They have become part of the landscape, to be expected in stressful careers. The problem is that we burn out. It is like a circuit breaker that switches off to prevent our brain from self-destructing. I have experienced this phenomenon personally. I had a nervous breakdown in 2004.

Fortunately, we can use techniques to turn off the Warrior that does not involve thinking. Ironically, we can't turn off the sympathetic nervous system by just thinking. In fact, we must stop thinking and let our brains reboot. Research by Dr. Stephen Porges and other neuroscientists has shown that activating our Vagus nerve turns off the Warrior and activates the parasympathetic nervous system, the Guru.

Here are recommended ways we can quickly and easily turn off the Warrior, relax, and return to positive experiences:

Smile:

When we smile, we move facial muscles in a way that activates the facial nerves connected to the C7 cranial nerve, which attaches to the Vagus nerve. Activating these facial nerves activates the Vagus nerve, and we feel relaxed. That is why it feels so good to smile.

Cold Water:

Splashing cold water on your face or taking a cold shower does wonders to reboot your mind. When you find yourself anxious, tense, stressed, or depressed, put cold water, a cold washcloth, or a cold towel on your face/head. You will feel better instantly.

Humming/Singing:

The vocal cords are situated near the Vagus nerve, and activating the vocal cords can activate the Vagus nerve, creating a feeling of relaxation and calmness. This is why singing and humming can be so satisfying. When you sing in the shower, there is a reason it makes us feel so good. When monks chant "OM," there is a reason that calms them down and clears their heads. These activities activate the Vagus nerve, resulting in calm and relaxation.

Hakalau:

Hakalau is a Hawaiian term that refers to "expanded vision." It is a technique developed by Huna healers in Hawaii to refocus the mind and create an "open mindedness" to allow the brain to create new neural pathways. It involves using peripheral vision to create new thought patterns.

Hakalau is extremely simple to achieve. Sit with your spine upright and looking straight ahead. Raise your hands with palms facing forward above your head. As you continue to look straight ahead, wiggle your fingers, and separate your hands until they are at the edge of your peripheral vision. Then raise and lower your hands along the edge of your peripheral vision as you wiggle your fingers.

You will notice an almost instant change in your mood and stress level. You will feel calm and relaxed. Continue to move your hands along the edge of your peripheral vision until you are free from anxiety and stress.

Eye movement:

When we move our eyes from the extreme left to the extreme right, we activate nerves connected to the C7 cranial nerve (see Smile above). Keeping the head upright and still, look as far to the left as possible for 60 seconds, then to the right for 60 seconds. When done correctly, you will yawn, signaling the Guru is activated.

There are other ways to activate the Vagus nerve, but these are the simplest and quickest ways to get results of relaxation and well-being. We should be doing these throughout the day, but at least whenever we feel the symptoms of the Warrior listed above. This way, you can feel relaxed and enjoy life again.

Much coaching attempts to train the mind to let go of negative thoughts, emotions, and beliefs so that our Guru can activate and bring our intuition and imagination into play. When we know that the Warrior is activated and follows the suggestions listed above, we can relax and start using the tools that coaching and marketing give us.

If we are not aware that the Warrior is activated, we do not relax; we do not use our intuition and imagination; we do not change. When you keep doing things the way you have always done, you will keep getting the results you have been getting. Albert Einstein said we can't change any problem with the same thinking that created it.

All the coaching and mentorship in the world will not help people who are chronically in Warrior mode. Getting into Guru mode is the only way to change your reality and results. Relax, calm down, and rationally problem-solve. In Guru mode, we can connect with other people, communicate, create and be civilized. We smile, we make friends, and we attract similar-minded people. Life becomes easy and effortless. This is the change we want.

***

To contact James:

Sir James Gray Robinson, J.D., Esq.

www.jamesgrayrobinson.com

info@jamesgrayrobinson.com

Angeline Mitchell

Angeline, a dedicated Women's Empowerment Partner, passionately supports survivors of domestic abuse on their journey to reclaim power and embrace love. Having navigated the challenges of leaving an abusive ex-husband, Angeline intimately understands the struggles these women face and is committed to offering guidance and a supportive community to help them thrive and Claim Victory.

The turning point in Angeline's life occurred when she courageously left her abusive relationship, transitioning from victim to victor. This pivotal moment ignited a personal growth journey where she crafted a new life plan and established a community founded on trust and security. Throughout this process, Angeline discovered the strength in unity, realizing she was not alone on her transformative path.

Having experienced the profound impact of mentorship and personal development, Angeline recognized the importance of sharing her powerful message with the world. Before doing so, she underwent the profound work of shedding limiting beliefs and dispelling the lies she had internalized over the years. This inner transformation allowed her to stretch beyond her comfort zone, guided by her unwavering faith, and fully embrace the life calling her.

Angeline's mission is clear: to empower and heal women worldwide who have endured domestic violence. She is dedicated to providing these women with the tools, resources, and unwavering support needed to reclaim their lives and thrive. Through the creation of an incredible community, Angeline aims to foster understanding, empathy, and upliftment, establishing a safe and nurturing space for healing and growth.

Who is Angeline?

By Angeline Mitchell

I was born and raised in Minnesota, worked in the family business, and went to college, yet I did not graduate as I had a mission and vision far greater than what my parents projected, so I made the move to New York in 1985.

My background is in sales and marketing in the advertising/direct mail industry. When I was very young, in my 20s, I thought I had met the love of my life, a very successful businessman who owned his own advertising/direct mail business. We married, and I soon became very successful, working in his business selling advertising/direct mail to businesses/restaurants in NYC, earning a six-figure income.

In September 2001, The World Trade Center collapsed. Business income fell 90% that year. While my husband chose to seek retirement, I set out to work in corporate America and proudly made a name for myself.

Sadly, my husband's face did not exude similar pride but rather only jealousy, resentment, and arrogance. I struggled with this issue for years. I feared bringing this to the attention of the New York State Police and authorities. He isolated me from my family and friends, denied me access to our banking accounts, insulted and demeaned me, humiliated me in public, and yes, he did strike and throw me against the wall in the middle of the night. I was hospitalized that night and subsequently had reconstructive nose surgery.

The list goes on and on. I realized I became the victim of physical and verbal assault and abuse, which continued for the next seven years.

In May of 2010, realizing that he had a slew of mental health issues and the verbal and physical abuse he heaped on me, I made the change and filed for divorce. I also had a court-ordered protective order for one year during my transition period. I was forced to leave my home many times and live in hotels and motels during this horrible time in my life. I lived on borrowed money from my parents. During this time, The New York State Police, The Dutchess County Sheriff, and the local authorities knew my whereabouts and were very supportive.

We all have choices. What a beautiful thing. I soon grew empowered to not only seek refuge and healing by surrounding myself with positive, outgoing, and caring people but also to inspire and support others to do the same. Relocating to Saratoga has captured this essence for me.

In October 2010, I decided to enter into the online space and joined a health and wellness company I was super passionate about. Coni Constantine, my upline 5-Star Diamond coach, contacted me about being a Team Beachbody Coach in the New York region. Realizing that I have a passion for health and fitness and want to inspire others to achieve their health and wellness goals, I joined Team Beachbody as a coach for six years.

While Team Beachbody was my steppingstone, I decided to leave this company because I had a vision and plan to help women who have suffered from domestic violence find their voice and empower them to step into their power and find their true purpose.

After leaving my abusive ex-husband, which was my first step to feeling FREE and transitioning from a victim to a victor in her life! She always says to have an exit plan, communicate with security, and don't do it alone! She started working in an advertising agency from 9 – 5. A lot of traveling was required in her position. Initially, it wasn't so bad, but it did become extraneous, which led her into the next phase of her life. Her job paid her a decent wage, but something inside her was seeking more than a decent wage. She knew she had a message to share with the world but just didn't know how to do it.

So I invested in a millionaire mentorship group. And it put her on a new path! Today, I am still invested in this group and have grown so many thanks to its mentors and amazing women (sisters!) who have shared and supported her goals to change the world.

I was growing slowly but learned that the hardest thing about growth is letting go of limiting beliefs.

Now I had to place myself in the hot seat by hosting webinars and doing Facebook Lives. Public Speaking is a big fear for everyone, and Angeline was no different! She had to tackle this as well. But her mentors and partners were by her side all the way, pushing her to be better.

I continued to surround myself with high-vibe individuals. Angeline began to experience tremendous personal and professional breakthroughs. She then started her coaching business, received invitations to speak on popular podcasts, and was a special guest last year on Inspired News Radio and the Women 4 Women Radio Network out of Canada. This year I was a special guest on the Pink Panther Podcast out of the U.K., Hot Topics the Podcast, and The Strong Enough Podcast Shows.

Angeline is a Women's Empowerment Partner dedicated to helping women who have suffered domestic abuse regain their power and acquire the necessary tools to heal and embrace goodness and love in their lives. Having experienced similar struggles, Angeline understands the journey firsthand and is determined to provide guidance and community so women can thrive and be victorious.

My mission is to empower and heal women worldwide who have experienced domestic violence, providing them with the tools, resources, and support they need to reclaim their lives and thrive. I am dedicated to creating an incredible community that understands, empathizes, and uplifts each other, fostering a safe and nurturing space for healing and growth.

Together, we are breaking the silence, shattering the stigma, and creating a world where survivors can heal, find their inner strength, and create a future filled with hope and possibility. I aim to impact 1000 women worldwide, empowering them to rewrite their stories and reclaim their power.

Together, we can create a ripple effect of healing, empowerment, and support that extends far beyond borders, inspiring and uplifting women from all walks of life. Join the movement and become part of a community that believes in the transformative power of healing and the strength that arises when women come together to support one another.

Inside the Let's Break the Silence Program, you'll be taken through my signature nine-step process designed to help you release and heal past wounds that have left you feeling overwhelmed, inferior, and lost. You will learn how to rediscover yourself and be empowered as you step into your divine power and identity that will lead you to your true purpose and calling in life, which God is calling towards.

My work now is having a huge impact on women. My Podcast Let's Break the Silence with Angeline has grown to 8 countries, with over 2000+ downloads with an average audience of 450+ per week. I have over 200 Episodes, and I am grateful for the opportunities this year to speak at a Live Virtual Speaking Summit Event for Women Coaches and Entrepreneurs called "Getting out of your own Damn Way," run by two amazing women with experience in the Public Speaking industry.

Here are some testimonials from my clients about my program:

Dawn Howell: "When I met Angeline a couple of years ago, I was instantly drawn to her spirit. She kept talking about limiting beliefs, and I didn't know what that meant.

It is because of her that my eyes were opened, and once I let go of my self-limiting beliefs, everything changed.

Thank you, Angeline. You are an amazing friend and an incredible sister in Christ.

I am so happy to be on this growth journey with you."

Dorinda Burke: I met Angeline through a mentoring program we were both involved in. We clicked instantly as we had the same perspective in life.

As I got to know Angeline better, I realized that she was on a mission to help women who have been domestic violence survivors.

Angeline is a kind, warm lady who has so much to give to the world. She is smart, intelligent, and a great leader. I am so honored to have her as my coach."

Alli MacDonald: "Angeline, helps with removing self-limiting beliefs, helps you define your worth, and makes it easy to do the homework. I enjoyed being a part of her masterclass so much!"

I am also a Board of Directors member for the Take Back the Night Foundation based out of Philadelphia, Pennsylvania, where I am in charge of the financial committee to raise funds for Sexual Violence victims.

Opportunities for future speaking events will be coming down the line for next year. I am also planning a Retreat with two other women entrepreneurs for next year at a location to be determined for next year in April of 2024.

I am honored and blessed to be part of the world's most relevant, fastest-growing personal development book series and co-author in the Change Book Series. My mission is to give women hope that we all have a voice for change and justice, as there are too many women out there who are seeking hope and wanting change so they can live the abundant life they truly deserve to live.

***

To contact Angeline:

My Website: https://www.letsbreakthesilence.com

My Social media links:

Facebook: https://www.facebook.com/angeline.constantinou/

LinkedIn: https://www.linkedin.com/in/angelinemitchell/

E-mail: angeline@letsbreakthesilence.com

Ana Smith

Throughout her global career, Ana Smith has been extremely curious about the impact and relationship between humans and technology, and for the past 25+ years, she's been part of executive, global teams in organizations such as Microsoft, General Electric, Hewlett Packard, and American Express, being involved in helping senior leaders within the organizations successfully execute on digital transformations and major organizational changes, helping teams, leaders and individual contributors elevate their performance and productivity, whilst optimizing their wellbeing. Leveraging technology, neuroscience, and adult learning principles to successfully operate at the crossroads of business, technology, and psychology.

Ana is also a highly sought after executive coach, speaker and facilitator noted for her passion for what she does and for her energizing and interactive style. She is the Chief Learning Officer of *Brightflare Performance Solutions.*

Ana wants to serve people and organizations as a leadership well-being strategist and coach by encouraging innovation and forward-thinking to inspire leaders, managers, and employees to be at their personal best to make the necessary organizational changes whilst finding personal fulfillment and meaning.

Change your Mindset, Change your Life."

By Ana Smith

I was born in Mexico City, one of the three largest cities in the world. I am the oldest of five children, raised in the suburbs within a household that was loving and caring in a unique way: my parents' way. My father grew a very successful business from the ground up – entirely on his own. His entrepreneurial spirit and corresponding achievements provided us with a comfortable life and great opportunities, always framed with these key values for his children: honesty, focus, hard work, intelligence, and formal education, the last of which my father didn't have. My mother is a loving, wonderful, and smart woman with an awesome sense of humor who has always been the glue of our family.

From a very young age, I was extremely observant and always curious as to why some people around me appeared so happy in their work, their lives, their jobs, their personal projects, and businesses, and others simply looked like they were ready to quit; they seemed to hate everything about their work and their lives in general. In these latter cases, you could see how their outlook on life showed in their demeanor, in their facial expressions, and in how they treated people around them. I later came to learn that it was their "mindset," which refers directly to the established beliefs, attitudes, and mental frameworks that shape an individual's perception, interpretation, and response to the world around them. In situations where individuals find themselves frustrated and fed up, shifting towards a growth mindset [1] —believing in the potential for change and actively seeking solutions—can be transformative. This shift can help them navigate challenges, take ownership of their circumstances, and ultimately find renewed satisfaction in their work, business, or their life in general.

The curiosity to understand this deeply intrigued me. What drives us to think and behave the way we do at work, with our families, and around others? Before starting undergraduate studies in Mexico City, candidates were given a whole vocational battery of tests, which were to be interpreted by one of the psychologists in the University's School of Psychology. In my case, the results were clear: at the early age of 18 years, I was told I had the "potential" to become a successful lawyer, mechanical engineer, or psychologist. I remember thinking, "I could not imagine myself as an engineer, yet my test results were brilliant. Did they get the right results?" To this day, I still smile when I remember this.

I chose to pursue a bachelor's in organizational psychology. This choice proved to be the right one for me. Yet, the curriculum lacked some of the more practical areas of well-rounded formal business topics encountered when becoming part of an organization. The basics of finance, operations, and marketing would have been beneficial. Even though the university I attended is considered one of the best in Mexico, even to this day, they missed that key piece of the puzzle. That taught me that there always needs to be a connection between the real world and formal education to be useful. Without it, you could potentially operate in a functional silo throughout your entire career if you fail to realize it quickly enough.

Here is my first key insight: We need to provide much more help and guidance to our high schoolers and undergrads on identifying their vocations and professions, considering that this is most probably what they will focus on for the rest of their lives. At those tender ages of 18 through 21 years, when the prefrontal cortex of the brain, vital for planning the future, impulse control, and decision making [3] is still not fully developed, who really knows what they want to do when "they grow up"? What gives them a direction or purpose in life, providing a sense of fulfillment to which they may take action, giving them satisfaction and a sense of meaning. This always reminds me of the Japanese term "Ikigai," which means "Iki" (to live) and" gai" (reason). Ikigai is similar in nature to the French term "raison d'etre" or "reason for being". It is a concept that has been rooted in the cultural fabric of Japan for centuries and simply means, "reason to live". Few things are more important than finding our reason for existing and being in life.

As the end of my undergraduate studies was fast approaching, I realized I wanted to work for big, global corporations. This triggered my thinking about which companies might fit the profile of the ideal employer that I was looking for. Therefore, in my last year at university, I realized during my internship that I needed to network and reach out to people, which is not an easy endeavor for an introvert. Yet I knew that no one was going to come and knock on my door and invite me to work at their global corporation if I didn't do my part first. This was one of the first times in my life that my own mindset was challenged. I didn't know it at the time, yet this is exactly what happened. I had to challenge my own attitude and beliefs and go out and network, so I did. Network, network, network; letting people know what I was after and what I had to offer: specifically, that I would give my 150%, that I'm a fast learner and am results and value-driven. I simply needed the opportunity to demonstrate what I was capable of. After several networking sessions, calls, coffees, and meet-and-greets, it worked! One of the people I networked with put me in contact with someone at American Express who was getting ready to leave. She was an internal recruiter responsible for recruiting for the company in all of Mexico! Long story short, I was one of ten candidates, including internal candidates, applying for a key role, and I got the job! This was the beginning of an extraordinary nine years at AMEX Mexico, including my last two as a senior sales manager, a promotion that I got – you guessed it – through people who I had worked with inside AMEX. These AMEX work associates knew me, liked my work, and trusted me as a team player and a professional. This helped me develop an ascending career in sales and human resources in other large, global organizations in Mexico and the US, including Citibank Merck, Bank of America, Hewlett Packard, General Electric, and Microsoft over 25+ years.

I continued to build my formal skill set through the attainment of a master's degree in organizational effectiveness at the University of Texas, as well as through multiple certifications that continued rounding out my expertise, my perspective, and my mindset inside organizations. I was fortunate to have met and coached thousands of amazing leaders in conjunction with their teams and traveled extensively, co-creating and executing high-impact, high-value senior development programs and learning experiences. However, I suddenly found myself at a crossroads. My elderly mother experienced an unfortunate fall and a subsequent fracture; this required around-the-clock personal care, love, and attention as she could no longer care for herself. This was the first time in my life that I had seen her so fragile, so much in need. Few people are prepared to take care of a loved one on a full-time basis. I certainly wasn't prepared. Not only did it require all of my time, attention, and care, but it also required my full emotional and physical resources.

Still working full-time, it was clear I needed to make a decision and move fast, very fast, in an effort to take care of her in this critical moment of need. I take this opportunity to acknowledge and recognize everyone who has had to make tough life-career decisions, especially those involving health issues, as well as acknowledge everyone who has ever been in a position to become a full-time caregiver with almost no planning or warning. Please accept my deepest empathy, respect, and love! I was fortunate to be there, to have a wonderful husband who supported and encouraged my decision and a family who was always willing to help. Not everyone has that.

This distinct situation required me to focus on my mother's health fully and presented me with an unplanned opportunity to completely disconnect from anything work-related for a year. During that period, I was able to reflect and focus on learning new skills, refreshing existing ones, and networking at an easy pace.

My husband started a successful boutique consulting firm in 2008 (Brightflare Performance Solutions), and that platform allowed me to start coaching executive private clients while also caring for my mother's needs. It also enabled me to bring my siblings into the mix in a more organized way to ensure that we all cared for her lovingly and allowed us to continue meeting our respective professional commitments.

During this period, I became inquisitive and interested in learning more about how our brain works, how mindsets are created, how thoughts affect emotions, how habits are formed, etc. The answer was to be found in neuroscience. Therefore, for the past decade, I have been studying and applying neuroscience-related topics through the lens of human behavior and well-being, both professionally and personally. I was very interested in trying to figure out how some people successfully change, learn, and evolve while others ruminate about what might have been, why are "they" and why not "me" getting the opportunities, the better life, the grand perks! I don't want to oversimplify neuroscience in the workplace, but I am fascinated by the fact that each one of us has the possibility to craft our own destiny through crafting our mindset. This may sound like an oversimplification, yet it is not. Neuroscience has advanced tremendously in the past 20 years, yet it is still in the process of fully understanding many of the intricacies and mysteries of the human brain. Yet this is where we are so far. What will the future bring in this regard?

Organizational culture, politics, favoritism, global economy, VUCA,[6] (Volatility, Uncertainty, Complexity, and Ambiguity), and other realities all exist in our world today; we cannot deny them. Yet, why is it that given these uncertainties, some people succeed, and others don't? Is it merely luck, chance, or being in the right place at the right time, or is it something else? Mindset is not limited to just growth mindsets and fixed mindsets [1]. These two categories can be on a spectrum, with individuals exhibiting elements of both fixed and growth mindsets in various aspects of their lives. It's also worth noting that mindset, the established beliefs, attitudes, and mental frameworks that shape anyone's perception, interpretation, and response to the world around them, is not a static trait; it can be cultivated and changed over time with self-awareness and deliberate effort. Amen to that!

I set out to answer this question, to understand how some people have their desires, the good, positive things they really expect to happen to them, and yet it is exactly the opposite for others. Could a person become successful at what they do and attain the things they dream about while others just get passed on? After deeply pursuing the topic, much personal reflection, and insightful interviews with experts in psychology, neuroscience, medicine, and spirituality, I have identified four key tenets that now guide my current work.

Firstly, to a large extent, we can create our own reality. According to Ramon y Cajal, Nobel Prize winner for medicine in 1906, "given the opportunity, every one of us could be capable of architecting our own brain/mind". Everything starts with our mindset. Our mindset, the lens through which we see the world, can shape our reality. It drives and influences our thoughts, feelings, and actions and ultimately determines the outcomes we experience. The first step towards changing your mindset is to acknowledge and embrace the power of beliefs. Henry Ford once said, "Whether you think you can or you think you can't, you're right." Your beliefs shape your reality. Beliefs are created and embedded in ourselves in infancy, during the first seven years of our life. They then become part of our subconscious and influence the shaping of our values.

Changing and understanding one's mindset and actively cultivating a growth-oriented perspective can profoundly impact individual performance, resilience, and adaptability. It empowers individuals to navigate obstacles, embrace change, and pursue their goals with a sense of possibility and optimism. It also requires a general understanding of how our brain operates in order for us to retrain it. It is important to understand that what each of us defines as "success" is not an overnight phenomenon; it is a journey. We must be prepared to face challenges, setbacks, and moments of doubt. But, in those moments, it's best to remind yourself of your purpose, reconnect with the belief in yourself, and press forward with unwavering determination. Believing in yourself, in your dreams, and in your ability to overcome any obstacles that come your way is key.

Thus, with mindset, everything starts with our beliefs, which instantaneously transcend into our thoughts, then firing up our emotions, which in turn will be followed by our actions.

Most people verbalize things without "really" wanting them to be true, yet they repeat them incessantly in their thoughts and in their self-talk. "I'm not good enough. I will never get that raise. I am never going to be able to leave this relationship." Such negative self-talk gives instructions to our subconscious. The conscious is instructing the subconscious on what to do; therefore, there is no surprise why we then fail.

There's another challenge. Many people don't understand why they don't get what they want or believe they deserve, mostly in part because they don't even really know what they want! In such cases, it becomes important to properly manage our focus and attention. Thoughts are the language of the brain; feelings are the language of the body, and how you think and feel creates a state of being. A state of being is when your mind and body work together, so your present state of being is your genuine mind-body connection.

The turning point in my life involving mindset happened a few years ago and started with a simple phone call.

Picture this: a typical evening, the digital grind in full swing, and a call from a dear colleague, we'll call her Sarah. My first instinct was to let it go to voicemail to keep my digital productivity on track. But something stopped me. I answered - and I heard Sarah's shaky, teary voice saying, "Ana, I'm not good enough, I'm not going to make it – and I know, I will miss something very important if I'm not always "on". I feel very, very lonely! Ana, please help me!" This hit me like a ton of bricks!

We rushed to the hospital. They took care of her almost immediately. After getting her diagnosis, in one of my follow-on visits to Sarah, she sheepishly shared with me her diagnosis: "the toll of extreme burnout, anxiety, depression and signs of cognitive decline". I thought to myself, 'Oh my God, if this could happen to Sarah it could happen to me.'

This rude awakening was a game-changer for me and fueled my personal journey. (Watch my TEDx on "How to foster well-being in the Digital Age").

My mission is simple: to improve our digital, emotional, and mental well-being through effectively changing our mindsets.

Secondly, rooted in research, I've identified a framework to promote the positive/good things you desire to happen to you! Like every formula, there are key ingredients that we need to know and master.

Recall that to change our mindsets, we need to understand some of the basic functions of the brain. Let's start with the *Reticular Activating System* (RAS) [3], which filters the unnecessary information from our sensory organs and allows the important information through into the mind/brain. The RAS also pursues data that validates your beliefs and connects the conscious mind with the subconscious mind [4]. Why is this important? Because when you identify what you want, what you really desire, this is the area of the brain that will start putting the relevant information in front of you. A simple example is a person who wants to buy a one-story home.

Once they define this desire, suddenly, it seems there are one-story homes available all around them. If you don't know what you really want, if you don't have a vision of what your desire could be, it is highly probable that key information related to what you want is simply passing you by.

The framework is direct: a) know yourself, learn how you respond to stress and life's challenges; b) learn how you manage your emotions (sadness, anger, wrath, etc.) in those moments when they are raw, and c) have a defined purpose for your life, which becomes key to align your goals and habits towards that purpose. A person without a life purpose or plan typically will jump to anything of interest almost immediately.

Thirdly, if what we aspire to is to fully understand how things work inside our mind, then acting upon that is even more important. With this knowledge, we can embark on a journey of transformation. I believe that every one of us has the power to change our lives.

A growth mindset is the foundation for personal and professional development. Suppose you embrace the belief that your abilities and intelligence can be developed through dedication, effort, and perseverance. In that case, you can challenge yourself to step out of your comfort zone, take risks, and continuously learn. With such a growth mindset, it becomes easier to view challenges as opportunities for growth rather than insurmountable obstacles.

To change your mindset, you must take ownership of your life. Stop playing the victim and start taking responsibility for your choices, actions, and outcomes. Understand that you have the power to shape your destiny. Remember, life may throw curveballs at you, but it is your response that will define your success. We can't change many aspects of the external environment; however, we can change how we respond to them. [5]

Fourthly, surround yourself with positivity. The people you surround yourself with greatly influence your mindset. Surround yourself with positive, supportive individuals who believe in your dreams and inspire you to become your best self. Seek out mentors, coaches, and role models who have achieved what you aspire to achieve. Their mindset and guidance will help propel you towards excellence. You will become the byproduct of the five people closest to you. If the five people closest to you have a victim mindset, don't be surprised if you develop a victim mindset. If the five people closest to you are successful executives, you will become the sixth.

In a world that seems to be hurtling forward at breakneck speed, I have worked very hard to become an empathetic and compassionate leader with a relentless passion for innovation in human behavior. This has me standing at the helm of a very exciting journey. My vision? To propel people and organizations across the globe into the future by embracing the awe-inspiring synergy of neuroscience and organizational psychology. Simply put, my mission is to improve our digital, emotional, and mental well-being.[7]

I have shared the latest groundbreaking research with many of my clients in one of my recent TEDx talks, co-presented with Colin Corby: *Are we losing our human identity to technology?* Colin has unveiled some of the secrets of neuroplasticity [2]—the brain's remarkable ability to rewire itself. This discovery holds the key to a fundamental truth: our mindsets are not fixed but instead malleable, opening up unprecedented opportunities for transformation.

As Tony Robbins famously said, "It's not the events of our lives that shape us, but our beliefs about what those events mean." I had to quickly underscore our mindsets' profound impact on our behavior, and my research continues to be an intricate part of the tapestry of the programs, retreats, and workshops I offer to my executive clients. My research paints a vivid picture of how understanding and reshaping neural pathways could revolutionize the way we work, lead, and live.

Drawing from researcher Brené Brown's expertise in vulnerability and storytelling, I have emphasized the power of narrative in shifting mindsets. Stories are the bridge to empathy, connecting us on a visceral level. They have the potential to dismantle barriers and facilitate profound change.

I would like to share a compelling success story of one of my clients, an ailing European manufacturing giant that underwent a transformative journey through the infusion of neuroscience-backed strategies.

Here's a summary of the key points:

My Client's Past: The company was once a leader but had fallen behind due to market changes. Silos had deeply formed, communication had broken down, innovation had stagnated, and morale and employee engagement were low.

My Approach: Introduce neuroscience-backed strategies to drive change from within. I emphasized the role of the brain's social circuitry to break down silos. A company-wide mindset shift program was initiated, leveraging neuroplasticity research, followed by a sustainability program to ensure constant improvement. Storytelling, as a new capability for leaders, played a crucial role in fostering cultural change.

The Transformational Result: Profits soared as a culture of innovative mindset flourished. The workforce became reinvigorated, reporting higher job satisfaction and engagement. The company gained an unassailable competitive edge, outpacing competitors in product development and efficiency.

This case study illustrates how the integration of neuroscience and organizational psychology can lead to remarkable transformations within organizations, propelling them toward enduring success in a rapidly changing business landscape.

Mindset transformation in my vision of the future is where organizations around the globe would not merely adapt to change but would thrive in its midst. My vision includes equipping these organizations with the cutting-edge strategies, tools, and tactics required for the future of work—where mindset shifts are the cornerstone of success.

Summarizing:

My Vision: Propel people and organizations across the globe into the future by embracing the awe-inspiring synergy of neuroscience and organizational psychology, equipping them with the cutting-edge strategies, tools, and tactics required for the future of work—where mindset shifts are the cornerstone of success.

My Mission: To educate people and organizations on how to best improve our digital, emotional and mental well-being.

My Future: To become a trusted advisor for leaders who truly care about their people, their well-being, and their outcomes, driving productivity in organizations across the globe.

My Passion: To change lives by positively changing mindsets.

How I Do It:

a. Speaking engagements: Keynote, single sessions or conferences – key topics: Well-being, Leadership, and Future of Work.

b. Introduce a new set of leadership and future work strategies to the world: presented through workshops, presentations, on-demand, and other forums as needed.

c. *Create and deliver executive retreats for leaders*: nurture leadership excellence and holistic well-being at exclusive retreats for Fortune 500 senior leaders, where visionary insights, peer connections, and cutting-edge strategies converge to shape the future of leadership and personal well-being).

d. *Seminars and workshops*: helping various stakeholders to improve upon their well-being and leadership through overall organizational change and sustainability outcomes.

e. *Private client coaching*: individual or group coaching, co-creating leadership philosophies, strategies, and flagship management and leadership development programs, including high-performing teams and other cutting-edge business themes.

If you'd like to connect with me or, better yet, work with me on the topics of mindset shifts, future of work, leadership, or well-being, I'd be honored and privileged to engage on a call and discuss the possibilities and options.

If you'd like to connect with me or, better yet, work with me on the topics of mindset shifts, future of work, leadership or wellbeing, I'd be honored and privileged to engage on a call and discuss the possibilities and options.

In conclusion:

In a world where agility and adaptability are non-negotiable, neuroscience is the compass that will guide us. It's time to rewrite our narratives, reshape our mindsets, and chart a course toward unparalleled success.

Remember, change starts from within. It begins with a decision, a commitment to yourself and your dreams. I urge every one of you to make that commitment. Decide to change your mindset and change your life. The journey may not always be easy, but the rewards will be immeasurable.

So, dare to dream big, think differently, and take bold actions. Embrace the challenges, learn from failures, and celebrate your successes. As you change your mindset, you will change your life, and in doing so, you will inspire others to do the same.

Remember: Change your mindset, change your life. Now, go out there and create the extraordinary life you deserve!

Thank you for your interest!

***

To Contact Ana:

Email: anasmith@brightflare.com

Website: www.brightflare.com

LinkedIn: www.linkedin.com/in/anasmithtalentstrategist

X (Twitter): https://twitter.com/anaismith

TikTok: https://www.tiktok.com/@yourprocoach_anasmith

Facebook : https://www.facebook.com/ana.smith.92372/

Instagram: www.instagram.com/anai_smith

REFERENCES:

[1] Dweck, Carol (2007) Mindset: The New Psychology of Success

[2] Puderbaugh, Matt; Emmady, Prabhu D., (2023) Neuroplasticity https://www.ncbi.nlm.nih.gov/books/NBK557811/#:~:text=It%20is%20defined%20as%20the,traumatic%20brain%20injury%20(TBI)

[3] Peters, Brandon M.D. (2022) Reticular Activating System and Your Sleep How Brain Disturbances Disrupt Sleep Patterns https://www.verywellhealth.com/definition-of-reticular-activating-system-3015376

[4] Reticular Activating System, Textbook of Clinical Neurology, Third Edition (2007)

https://www.sciencedirect.com/topics/veterinary-science-and-veterinary-medicine/reticular-activating-system

[5] Frankel, Viktor (2006): Man's Search of Meaning

[6] Nate Bennett and G. James Lemoine (2014) "What VUCA really means for you"

https://hbr.org/2014/01/what-vuca-really-means-for-you

[7] Dingman, Marc PhD (2019) "Your Brain Explained"

https://www.amazon.com/Your-Brain-Explained-Neuroscience-Reveals/dp/1473696550/ref=sr_1_1?keywords=marc%20dingman&qid=1569319022&refinements=p_85%3A2470955011&rnid=2470954011&rps=1&s=books&sr=1-1

[8] Smith, Ana and Corby, Colin (2023) TEDx: Are we losing our human identity to technology?

Carla Michelle Hooker

Carla Michelle Hooker, a dedicated dance educator and passionate advocate for children, hails from Washington, DC, and Prince George's County, MD. Her love for dance blossomed during her formative years at the esteemed Art Linkletter Totten Dance Studio, where Miss Dolly Austin served as her guiding force.

Following her studies at East Carolina University, Carla took a momentous step in 1990 by establishing Karla's Kids Musical Ministries. Through this initiative, she has imparted the art of dance to numerous children, bringing joy and transformation to their lives, particularly in inner-city and rural communities.

Carla's unwavering commitment to her craft and her students has opened doors to remarkable opportunities. Her profound passion for children, combined with her ability to inspire and uplift, has left an indelible mark on the lives of countless young individuals earning her an honorary doctorate in Humanitarianism. Through her faith-based approach, she empowers children to utilize their God-given talents and love for dance, paving the way for a brighter future.

As an exceptional leader, mentor, role model, and mom to her daughter Kamaria, Carla's dedication and unwavering support for children have made her a beacon of hope. Her journey stands as a testament to the transformative power of dance and the enduring spirit of hope

Adversity to Strength: Unveiling Resilience

By Carla Hooker

In my childhood, I was fortunate to be raised in a household with two parents, just like many of my best friends. I was able to see my parents' leadership styles and gain valuable lessons. My mother, a passionate teacher, took on her role passionately and enthusiastically. She also displayed a firm but compassionate demeanor. My father, who was a desk sergeant in an inner-city police department, displayed a leadership style that was firm yet empathetic towards his prisoners.

Their collective influence taught the importance of dedication and passion, treating everyone with dignity, and giving back. Their efforts to help the less fortunate have left a lasting impression, influencing my beliefs and inspiring me to follow their example.

As a young child, I was persistent and outgoing, eager to help my family, teachers, and classmates. I found it deeply satisfying to help others. As I entered kindergarten, however, the pressure of conforming to social expectations affected my self-esteem and spirit. My innate intelligence and desire to help others often caused me to be isolated from my peers.

As a result of my intelligence and ability to finish tasks before schedule, I could not resist the urge to assist my classmates. This only isolated me further. I was in a world of my own, struggling with my thirst for knowledge. My kindergarten teacher was frustrated by my desire to help and moved me behind her desk to hide me from the other students.

Isolation allowed me to reflect upon the complexity of my journey. Intelligence and isolation interacted, forming my future path. I remember being disappointed when I was told I couldn't help my classmates. My mother insisted that I should be given more complicated tasks. However, my teacher allowed me to help her only reluctantly.

My parents instilled in me the value of exploration and exposure to new experiences. They introduced me to a wide array of activities and interests. My mother and father provided unwavering support, nurturing my curiosity for the arts. They introduced me to classical instruments, museums, theater, fine dining, family vacations, participation in organizations like Girl Scouts and Girl in Action Junior Missionaries, and various forms of dance, among other things. Out of all these experiences, dance emerged as my true passion. As I contemplate my life's journey, I find myself pondering the future and reflecting on my childhood aspirations. During my formative years, I idolized figures such as Diana Ross and Cher. Their stylish, glamorous outfits, distinctive hairstyles, and refined demeanor greatly inspire me. I also profoundly admired characters like Isis, Wonder Woman, and the Bionic Woman.

Isis fascinated me with her spiritual strength and unwavering faith, which she used to overcome life's challenges. Wonder Woman, with her strength and truth-revealing lasso, captivated me. Her invisible jet and bullet-blocking bracelets showcased her fearlessness. The Bionic Woman's story of resilience, having undergone numerous surgeries and rebuilding her strength, left a lasting impression on me. She was resourceful and unwavering in the face of adversity.

As I reflect on my life's aspirations, I find myself asking who I aspire to be like and who I genuinely admire. These influential figures from my childhood serve as a source of inspiration and guidance and tap into why it's not only important for me to be totally authentic but also for YOU to be true to who you really are. Yes, it's okay to be assisted and trained by those who can help us, but it's up to you and me to use what we already have between our two ears and feel in our hearts and souls to become who we were designed to be. Look in the mirror and ask yourself, who am I? What do I want? Why am I here? I do this and try to be completely honest with myself. I've noticed that the more transparent I become with myself, the less I hold myself back, work on what needs to be improved, and keep pressing forward. Try it now. See how sincere you can be with yourself and work on improving your goals and areas in your life where change is necessary in a positive way, not beating yourself up.

Both my mother and father, who were aware of the importance of nurturing my artistic and intellectual interests, enrolled me at an early age in dance classes. My dance teacher, Mrs. Dolly Austin, guided me on a journey of transformation that had a profound impact on my self-confidence. The unwavering encouragement, mentorship, and optimism of Mrs. Austin became the basis for my personal growth. She consistently praised me, regardless of my technical ability, and instilled an unwavering confidence in my abilities.

I enjoyed ballet and tap dance classes immensely during my time in dance school. I found acrobatics more difficult. As I approached the age of eleven, my commitment and seriousness to my dance training increased. Inspired by my cousin Joyce, who excelled in dance, I was determined to improve my technique and follow her example.

Joyce's talents and accomplishments were a great source of inspiration to me. I wanted to be like her and develop my talents to impact the dance world.

After completing the training required for en-pointe dancing, I began experiencing severe leg pains. I also noticed swelling in my feet and legs. My parents were worried and took me to my pediatricians, who agreed that my rigorous training had taken a toll. I was not convinced by their opinion and sought a second opinion at Children's Hospital. Unfortunately, they all came to the same conclusion. Not only was I told not to continue pointe classes, but also that I couldn't dance anymore. The news was devastating. I tried to negotiate with my parents and the doctors but without success.

After that, I was forced to take pain medications at school. I also had to leave the classroom frequently to drink water and go to the bathroom. The school nurse would always be vigilant and come to me to draw attention to my medical conditions. I was annoyed by the attention and kept a low profile in class to avoid it. I sacrificed my personal growth and identity to blend in.

I continued to shrink myself throughout my life. This was especially true during childhood when conformity and acceptance were expected. To gain approval and not upset others, I suppressed many of my desires and needs. In addition to my battle with sickle disease and sickle arthritis, I felt different because I was frail and thin and wore thick glasses. Due to chronic fatigue and brain fog, I couldn't keep pace with my peers in school. I felt isolated in college and, as an adult, unable to participate in the activities of others. Even though it was never normal, I thought this was my destiny. My doctors warned me I may not live beyond 18 or 21, but I miraculously survived. What have you miraculously survived? How did you do it?

Has anyone ever put limitations on you? How did it make you feel? Do you ever feel frustrated or left out? When were you ever told that you couldn't do something you were passionate about? Did you persevere? Or did you decide to fold under pressure? Did you accept failure or disappointment as a learning experience and move forward?

I felt a spirit of hope and determination emerge within me. It was like a phoenix emerging from the ashes. I promised not to let anyone's opinions or limitations stop me from pursuing my dreams. Despite my debilitating illness, which stole away my passion for dance and my childhood, and the freedom that my cousin, a ballerina, and other children enjoyed outside, I was determined not to let anyone's opinion or limitations stop me from achieving my dreams. I spent my school days in the nurse's room, hydrating constantly and dealing with chronic pain and fatigue. My blood disorder caused me to suffer excruciating pain. I was forced to use crutches, not because of broken bones but due to the intense pain. I felt my heart and soul shattered but refused to let that define me. Have you ever been through something that broke your heart or soul?

While I was struggling with both emotional and physical setbacks in school and dance, an even bigger storm brewed at home that shattered the image of my happy family. My grandfather took his life shortly after my parents divorced, during my final year in elementary school. I was overwhelmed and stuck in a more resounding silence.

I didn't always sit on the sidelines. At times, I pushed myself as hard as I could to prove not only to myself and my parents but also to others that I possessed more strength than they gave me credit for. My journey started in elementary school when I began learning to play the flute. In music class, I met Michelle Johnson, who is now a Grammy Award-winning artist. We both lived in Birchwood City,

Oxon Hill, Maryland. Unfortunately, our first school music teacher had a habit of throwing erasers and chalk at us, behaving like he was having temper tantrums. His outbursts occurred whenever someone played the wrong note or didn't hold the note for the designated amount of time. Despite his shortcomings, we aimed for perfection to avoid his fits of rage and managed to become skilled players.

From a young age, I learned the importance of resilience, self-determination, and the power of faith to navigate life's challenges. We all encounter difficult and unexpected experiences, but it's crucial not to be consumed by them. Some people become stuck in the aftermath of a challenging event, existing rather than truly living. They park themselves in a state of dormancy, allowing their dreams to wither away. Regrettably, many never reclaim their true destiny because they fail to overcome obstacles that appear more daunting than they are.

Later, in junior and senior high school, I played in the orchestra. I was skilled in playing both the flute and the bassoon. Playing these instruments, like my passion for dance, allowed me to escape into my world for a few hours alone in my bedroom. I would also get lost in the pages of my encyclopedias. Opening my Britannica and World Books, I would embark on imaginary journeys to Indonesia, Vietnam, Japan, Rhodesia, Egypt, France, and all over the United States. I dreamt of visiting places like the Midwest, the West Coast, Alaska, and Maine—states that I had never been to with my parents. As a child, tween, and teen, I had a vivid imagination, and my father often referred to me as a hermit because I found solace and peace in my room alone. He believed it wasn't healthy for me to spend so much time in isolation, but I never felt lonely. I had my dreams and goals to keep company.

In junior and senior high school, I also had the opportunity to join the yearbook club, which I absolutely adored because I had a passion for writing. I had already written two books during elementary school, although they were never published. The first book was about different birds, and I even illustrated it myself. Although my first-grade teacher criticized me for writing too large and struggling with a regular pencil due to my sickle cell pain, I was still proud of my creation. The second book, written in fifth grade, focused on raccoons, and I had my older cousin Karen illustrate it for me.

I learned many valuable lessons from my struggles that have helped me in adulthood. These include resilience, strength, compassion, faith that never wavered, and a profound understanding that I can shape the life that I want and help others who are experiencing similar sadness and chaos. As a child, I realized that you have the power to create the life you desire. This was a revelation I came to while dealing with the stress and unpredictable nature of sickle-cell disease. You have a unique essence that is different from everyone else's. It's vital to reconnect with this essence. Close your eyes and think back on the events in your life that have left an impression on you. What were you feeling at that time? We all have the inner strength to change our lives, no matter what. It's for this reason that I decided to teach children to dance and be a coach.

Dance is an empowering vehicle for the mind, spirit, and body. Dance builds self-esteem and confidence. It allows individuals to find freedom and transformation through their artistry. I began my dance journey as a young girl with a lot of energy who could not sit still. My parents saw my unbridled energy and decided to enroll me in dance lessons as a way of expressing myself. This was a far cry from my daydreams when I became a star on my stage. Inspired by Diana Ross and Cher and using a blanket or towel as flowing hair, I imagined being in the spotlight with an imaginary microphone made from an afro-pic hair comb. These moments of pretending ignited an inner fire that shaped my life. Little did I realize that my introduction to dance led me to Arthur Mitchell, the co-founder of Dance Theater of Harlem, who helped make my dream of opening my dance studio a reality.

In high school, I experienced a major shift when I discovered that I had an entrepreneurial spirit. My stepmother, who I call Mommy, was a constant presence in my life. She ignited this newfound passion. She worked from home as a medical and legal transcriptionist while fulfilling her role as a stay-at-home mother. Even before I started preschool, the seeds of my desire to be a dance instructor with my studio were planted. My aspirations intensified throughout middle and high school, eventually transforming into a burning desire to open my own studio. My college and high school friends may have grown tired of hearing me discuss my dream. It was my unwavering resolve that slowly transformed this dream into reality.

I decided to leave college because of illness. In my new job, I started working with children, and I was able to fulfill my dreams. My cheerleading squad became my first dancers, and I formed a traveling dance troupe. My dream was born. Influential figures such as the Mayor of DC, former Mayors, Commissioners for the Arts and Humanities, local TV and radio stations, Rabbis, Pastors, and Arthur Mitchell, along with his renowned dancers, recognized our achievements at the Duke Ellington School of the Arts. Even Mr. Mitchell and his former assistant from the John F. Kennedy Center for the Performing Arts awarded me a full scholarship.

In my early years of education, I acquired a wide range of skills. My mother instilled in me a love of fashion and self-expression. Her confidence and impeccable style left me with a lasting impact. I was dressed to the nines in the latest fashion trends and looked like a miniature version of her. When I expressed an interest in modeling, my stepmother, with her professional experience in New York City, became a valuable coach. She gave me the necessary training and knowledge to help me pursue my modeling dreams. My stepmother, mother, and father all worked together to help me achieve my dreams. They even helped me participate in a professional model search. One such event was held in the DC region at a venue that Herb, an ex-R&B singer and former police officer, owned. In college, I honed my modeling skills and was eventually accepted into prestigious modeling groups such as Ebony's Fashion Fair, John Casablanca's Model Talent Management, etc.

My experiences and unique skills have given me a toolkit of versatile tools. I can now coach and mentor young talent in many areas, such as modeling, dance, performance, media interviews, and public speaking. My journey taught me about the power of following your passions and how resilience is essential in the face of adversity.

While I possess talents in several other areas, dance remains the medium that fills my heart with music and feels like my calling. I derive immense joy and fulfillment from teaching children and adults how to use their bodies as a means of self-expression, providing them with a sense of freedom and creativity within a specific time and space.

As a result of my vast experience, I've had the honor of helping countless boys and girls achieve their dreams. Together, we have won talent contests, received scholarships, and won local, national, and global pageants. It is a rewarding journey that allows me to share the knowledge and experience I have gained through the many opportunities I've been fortunate to pursue.

I hope the stories from my life shared in this chapter of the book will encourage you to reflect on your fond childhood memories. The lessons we needed to thrive in adulthood were imparted to us through our childhood experiences, whether positive, negative, or neutral.

Over the past three decades, I have had a positive impact on the lives of thousands of inner-city and rural children and teenagers. By designing my program, I was able to improve the outcomes of youth who were at risk. Karla's Kids Dance, my faith-based programs, systems, and protocols, have helped to deter children from drug abuse, violence, crime, and delinquency. This includes children who live in inner cities, rural areas, and suburbs. My program has taught children how to use their God-given talents, intelligence, and passion through dance.

***

To contact Carla:

karlaskidsdance@gmail.com

carlahookerauthor@gmail.com

(919)842-8154

Rachel Best

Rachel is a keynote motivational speaker, founder of How to Make Your Mark in the World, and author, podcaster, and empowerment mindset coach.

She is the owner of a personal development company as a Certified Neuro-linguistic Empowerment Mindset coach. She is also certified in Timeline Therapy. She helps her clients overcome mindset blocks and limiting beliefs to identify what is holding them back from walking in their true purpose and potential, to let go of what is holding them back, to reprogram their minds, and to make big moves in their life.

Her passion is to awaken individuals in how to make their mark in the world, find their signature, and use their gifts, talents, and life experiences.

Rachel is Married with five kids ranging from 7-25 and has two grandsons.

Her favorite things to do are to be with family and to travel the country. In September 2021, her husband Josh, youngest son Maverick, and Rachel decided to sell their home to live full-time in their RV.

Being by the ocean, palm trees, and sun fills her soul.

From Dreamer to Achiever
Making a Mark in the World

By Rachel Best

"Your message has the power to change lives, and it is up to you to take it to the world, To Make Your Mark in the World. You get to decide how this will happen." – Rachel Best

When I was a young girl in my hometown of Delphos, Ohio, a community of fewer than 7000 people, I had a big dream and vision for life—growing up in a quiet town where not much happened, surrounded by fields and forests. For as long as I can remember, I was curious about the world beyond this small town. My imagination took me to places I had never been, and I dreamed of seeing the bright lights of big cities and experiencing diverse cultures. I daydreamed about traveling to different locations while taking in all the sights and sounds.

As a little girl in my bedroom playing with Barbie dolls' hair, I was filled with a dream that I would do hair and makeup. I wanted to do celebrities' hair in Hollywood. But life took an unexpected turn when I became pregnant and then a mother as a sophomore in high school at 17 to my first-born son Devin. As you can only imagine, many looked down upon my situation, but by God's grace, I not only graduated high school with an 18-month child on my hip, but I also earned my cosmetology license. Despite the challenges, I refused to give up on my dreams.

My parents always said I was rebellious and pushed against the grain. They called it "rebellious." I saw it as "determination." All I knew was that I wanted to accomplish great things in life. My hope was to make what I saw in my mind and felt in my heart. I became a great multitasker. All the while, I worked nearly full-time for a fast-food restaurant while staying in school and raising a baby. Devin, his father, and I lived at my parents' house throughout my junior year of high school. By my mid-senior year, we were able to get a small apartment near my parents.

After high school, I married my high school boyfriend, Devin's father. By the age of 22, I had three children, all under the age of five. We were a struggling young family trying to pay all the bills, diapers, formula, and handle babysitting. Can you imagine the stress that added to life? Knowing we needed more space, we moved to a village named Spencerville in Ohio. We went from a tiny town to an even smaller one with only one stoplight. I knew I had to do what it took to survive, so I started working as a makeup artist and hair stylist at a hair salon. During this time, we were so poor that we had no other alternative but to live on government assistance.

During my 7th year of marriage, my life took a turn when I came home from work to an empty house. My husband left and never returned. There was no goodbye. I was faced with the reality that I would raise our three children alone. This was the darkest time in my life. I found myself abandoned, depressed, and afraid of the unknown future I was forced to walk through. I had never planned it this way. I just knew his decision changed my and my three children's lives forever.

Soon after, I found myself making decisions I would regret. Once again, I found myself making a decision that would drastically alter my story, which would ultimately become my life's purpose. This pivotal moment shaped my journey and inspired me to share my story through my book "How to Make Your Mark in the World…Finding Your Signature."

On March 18, 2009, I had an encounter with Jesus, the one who would transform my life. From that day on, I have meditated on the Bible to teach and guide me. This is how my transformation has come to pass. My hope is to carry this decision with me for the rest of my life. I started saying "yes" to Jesus, one "yes" at a time. Through this, I have listened to His calling on my life and the obedience that has led me to go where He guides me and do what he asks. I find comfort in the bible verse:

The Change[20]

1 Thessalonians 5:16-18 says, "Rejoice always, pray without ceasing, give thanks in all circumstances; for this is the will of God in Christ Jesus for you."

Being a single mother was demanding. There were many obstacles I would need to overcome as it was a daily challenge. I understand that the road was a long, winding one that ultimately tested my strength, courage, and resilience. During those years, I lacked self-esteem, confidence and often found myself alone and overwhelmed trying to be both mom and dad to my children. At times I would want to give up, but the hope in reading the Word of God would give me the strength to push forward. I had faith that if I stayed true to God's calling, He would honor His promises. The blessing would come five years later, and I would meet my forever love. We became a blended family.

During the Spring of 2015, I found a health and wellness company that introduced me to Mindset and Personal Development. Besides my faith and the Bible, I had never been inspired and challenged to grow. I was never much of a reader in my younger years, as that was a challenge for me. In fact, the last books I read were those I had to read during my high school years. I knew this would not be easy; nevertheless, I accepted the challenge. I started digging into personal development books. Luckily this time, we had new technology in the world that allowed me to dive into audiobooks, YouTube, and podcasts. I discovered a new part of my life that I began to fall in love with, which helped me learn and grow.

Four years later, I attended a leadership summit that would change my life forever. While there, I heard God speaking to me. He told me that I needed to quit my hairstylist job and that I needed to pursue coaching full-time. I found myself at a crossroads. I loved my job as a hairstylist but knew God was calling me to do something bigger and greater. I remember several years before, when I got saved, I knew I would be sharing my testimony on a public stage someday. I was given a vision that I would become a public speaker who would inspire others to overcome obstacles, accomplish their dreams, and find their purpose.

I've always had big dreams. I refused to let what others told me "you can't" stop me from becoming the person I was created to be. The words "you can't" fueled me to prove them wrong. I would not let the narrative of "what not to be like" become a reality, but rather the story of redemption and who God created me to become. I knew I had to pursue my dreams, so I quit my full-time salon job of 20 years and decided to go all-in with the personal development, health, and wellness company. This was the vehicle that provided me the financial freedom to be at home with my family, along with the time that has allowed me to grow and learn in my faith and personal development.

As I dove deeper into pursuing personal development, I wanted to find the solutions and reasons why people get stuck. I became proficient in the understanding of our conscious and unconscious minds; in this, I found the pathway to get unstuck in all areas of one's life. I found an incredible program that would ultimately serve as the key to what I had been searching for.

As I began learning more about the factors that keep us from achieving our goals and how we can overcome limiting beliefs and traumas, I realized that my true calling was to help others do the same. Shortly before starting my certification classes, I envisioned a bicycle pedaling while shifting gears and then coming to an abrupt stop. Suddenly, the bike started to clunk and gain momentum once again. I heard God telling me that we were shifting gears. At that time, I had no idea what this meant, but over the next year and a half, it became abundantly clear that my next chapter in life was to launch my own Personal Development coaching business, become a paid speaker and author of many books. I would get to travel the world and pursue the dreams that had been stirring up inside of me for some time.

In 2021, I began speaking on stages, and it became clearer to me that my vision to become a keynote motivational speaker was becoming my reality. I can remember there was a very brief moment when I felt like I had missed the mark. After making endless phone calls to secure speaking engagements, I faced rejection after rejection and began to doubt myself. Once again, I turned to God, praying and seeking guidance about my next steps. One day I was working out while listening to Les Brown for inspiration. At that moment, I felt like he was speaking directly to me. In his words, I felt an overwhelming peace that confirmed speaking was my calling. I knew with certainty that I was on the right path. Looking back, I feel as if my faith was testing my commitment to push forward or give up.

The next day, to my surprise, a Facebook friend whom I had never met before reached out to me to connect on the phone. I received an invitation to be a part of his speaker comp. And I said yes. Leaving this competition, I left inspired. Weeks later, I was part of a mastermind that moved me to fully commit to focusing on making my mark with my story. Everything started to fall into place when my goal was to become a successful speaker.

My heart's desire is to share my story with many so that they, too, believe whatever they decide to commit to can come to fruition. It is not easy, as I have spent countless hours understanding and developing my message so that you would understand how you can have the same opportunity I have been given. My goal is to continue speaking on local to global platforms and virtual conferences, along with challenging myself to participate in speaker competitions and academies. My hope is to inspire individuals to overcome their setbacks in life while giving them hope and inspiration.

Many people carry their purpose, as I would say, in a backpack rather than in their heart. I have created a course to teach people how to "Make their Mark in the World." They will find their purpose using their gifts, talents, and life experiences. This course is designed to help individuals identify their passions and develop a plan to achieve their goals. In there, you will find tools for public speaking, crafting your message, and sharing it. You will learn all of the tools needed to succeed. In addition to the course, there will be speaking events and platforms worldwide by which all speakers will come together to share their passion for making a difference in the world as thought leaders. I aim to awaken the voice within, even those who did not know they had a story to share.

My ultimate vision is to have a non-profit that will host small intimate events that will awaken people to see their dreams as reality. My dream is to buy a house on the beach so I can invite others to experience growth and empowerment.

Did you know that our life, when transformed, can be much like the process of refining gold? Just as gold needs to be melted down and purified to become valuable, we, too, may need to go through a transformation process to reach our full potential. This process can involve breaking down old habits, beliefs, and behaviors that no longer serve us and replacing them with new ones that align with our values and aspirations.

Just as gold is heated to high temperatures to separate it from impurities, we may need to face intense challenges or difficult situations to shed our own negative qualities and become the best versions of ourselves. This process can be painful and uncomfortable, but it is necessary for personal growth and transformation. As gold is refined and transformed into something beautiful, we can emerge from our refining process as a more authentic, resilient, and fulfilled version of ourselves. This transformation can lead to greater joy, meaning, and purpose in our lives as we align with our true selves and live in harmony with our values.

A simple exercise to find your number one goal:

Write down five things you are passionate about. Now cross out two, now cross out two more. The remaining is your number one dream, goal, or desire. This is the motivating factor that will take you where you want to go. As you focus on just that one goal, the other goals will naturally fall into place.

1_____

2_____

3_____

4_____

5_____

5 Keys To Elevate Your Success:

1. Forgive and let go: Forgive yourself and others who have hurt you in the past. Holding grudges and resentments can hold you back from success.

2. Follow your path: Obey and follow the direction that God takes you. Trust that your path will lead you to your purpose.
3. Believe in yourself: Have faith and belief in yourself, and trust that what you hope for is achievable. Believe until you see the results you desire.
4. Commit and take action: Make a commitment to your goals and take action towards achieving them every day. Go all-in and take at least one step every day to move towards your goals.
5. Invest in yourself: Prioritize your personal and spiritual growth by investing in yourself first. Surround yourself with growth-minded people, hire a coach to guide you, and clean up any negative programming in your mindset that may be holding you back.

Additionally, tell everyone about your dreams and goals, as speaking them out loud can make them a reality.

Remember we get to choose in life how we are going to make an impact.

Your message has the power to change lives, and it is up to you to take it to the world, To Make Your Mark in the World.

**

To contact Rachel:

Facebook: Rachel Best

https://www.facebook.com/iamrachelbest

Instagram: @iamrachelbest

LinkedIn: Rachel Best

Websites:

Rachelbestspeaks.com

Iamrachelbest.com

Nicole Harvick

Nicole Harvick is known as The Quantum Energy Healer and Forgiveness Expert because she can help you find and release old traumas that are stuck in your body. An example of what she has achieved is helping a 55-year-old woman find the exact moment she felt unworthy and unloved. The woman was just 18 months old when the trauma occurred.

Her passion is forgiveness, and she is now on a mission to help others understand and practice forgiveness in their own lives. Her desire is to help as many people as possible to utilize forgiveness to help them walk their path free of any negative emotions or pain that resides in their body.

Nicole is certified in many healing modalities including Usui Reiki, Tuning Fork Therapy, Quantum Energy Healing and is a certified Ho'oponopono EFT Practitioner.

She is also certified to facilitate meditation and does that both in person and online.

Nicole is the designer and creator of The Ho"oponopono Bracelet.® This is a line of both men and women's bracelets which are infused with reiki energy, prayer and sound.

Nicole the is the author of several books including,

Boy on a Swing" 2018

The Gift of Forgiveness 2019

The Alchemy of Forgiveness 2021

1% More 2022

Nicole resides in South Carolina where she enjoys days at the beach along with kayaking, paddleboarding, yoga and meditation.

Living Beyond the 3rd Dimension

By Nicole Harvick

My journey of spirituality started for me as a child. I did not really understand what spirituality or spirits were, but I often had vivid dreams in which I was being strangled. I once woke up and was pulling something off my throat. I held seances as a child. I read every book I could find about the spirit world. As I reflect, I now know this was always my path to walk.

I have always had Clair abilities, with my strongest being Clairaudient, which is the ability to hear and receive messages.

When I started writing the chapter for this book, I was going to write about forgiveness and self-love. This is a subject that I write, teach, and speak about. However, as I neared the completion of my chapter, I received a message from my spirit guides. They said to me, Same Content, Same Outcome.

Knowing this was a message, I asked them what they wanted me to write about. The answer was that they were asking me to write about my journey from existing in a 3rd-dimensional reality to thriving in a 5th-dimensional timeline. I always know it's best to listen to my guides and intuition.

Let's begin with an explanation of what the 3rd dimension is.

Living in a 3rd-dimensional reality can be challenging to comprehend, especially if unfamiliar with the concept. The third dimension is the physical plane of existence, characterized by length, width, and height. It is the reality we experience in our daily lives, and most people believe this to be the only reality that exists. However, a few signs indicate when we are living in a 3rd-dimensional reality.

Firstly, the sense of separation is a sign of living in a 3rd-dimensional reality. This separation is often a feeling of disconnection from others, nature, and the universe. People living in a 3rd-dimensional reality typically feel alone in an unresponsive world. They feel that everything is separate from them, and they have difficulty seeing how everything is connected.

Another sign of living in a 3rd-dimensional reality is a focus on physicality. In this reality, physicality is seen as the only reality, and everything is judged based on physical appearance. People living in a 3rd-dimensional world often judge others based on their physical appearance, believing that the physical world is all there is to life. This attitude often leads to a lack of spiritual growth and personal development, as they fail to see beyond the physical.

A third sign of living in a 3rd-dimensional reality is a belief in linear time. The notion of time is seen as something that can never be changed, and everything is expected to progress linearly and predictably. People believe that time is something that is fixed, and nothing can be done to alter it. This belief often leads to a rigid mindset, where people refuse to consider that there are other ways of viewing time.

Finally, focusing on material wealth signifies living in a 3rd-dimensional reality. People often believe having money and material possessions is the key to happiness and success. As a result, they are often obsessed with acquiring more things and competing with others in a never-ending cycle of accumulation. Unfortunately, this attitude often causes people to neglect other areas of their lives, such as relationships, spirituality, and personal growth. These signs often lead to an unfulfilling life where people cannot see beyond the physical world.

Several energy blocks can occur in this frequency; one of them is the ego. This seems to be the one thing many people will fight to hold onto.

Transcending the ego is a topic that has interested spiritual seekers and thinkers throughout history. The ego is our sense of self, identity, thoughts, and emotions. It is the lens through which we experience the world. However, it can also be a source of suffering, causing us to become attached to our thoughts, feelings, and gains or losses.

Therefore, transcending the ego means letting go of these attachments and experiencing a sense of freedom and peace that goes beyond the ego.

In a 3rd dimensional reality, ego can play a significant role in how people interact with each other. It can cause them to become defensive, competitive, and even hostile towards each other. This can result in a lack of cooperation and collaboration, making it more difficult to achieve common goals.

Moreover, ego can also impact one's perception of reality. People with high levels of ego are often fixed in their ideas and beliefs, making it difficult for them to consider other perspectives. This can lead to an inability to adapt to changing circumstances and resistance to new experiences and knowledge.

The first step in transcending the ego is to become aware of it. We need to learn to recognize the ego's voice, which often encourages us to maintain our sense of self and identify with our desires, fears, and insecurities. This means we must be mindful of our thoughts, feelings, and reactions and acknowledge them without judgment. This self-awareness enables us to separate ourselves from our ego and observe it objectively.

The next step is to question the ego's assumptions. We need to ask ourselves if our beliefs and desires are necessary or if they are the product of conditioning, desires, or fear. For example, we may feel that we are not good enough unless we achieve a certain status or have a certain amount of money. However, this belief may not reflect reality and only create unnecessary suffering. We can free ourselves from our assumptions and beliefs and experience a sense of liberation by questioning our assumptions and beliefs.

Transcending the ego requires self-awareness, questioning assumptions, and developing compassion and empathy. It is a process that cannot be achieved overnight but requires consistent effort and practice. However, the rewards of transcending the ego are worth it - we can experience a sense of connectedness with others and a deep sense of inner peace that goes beyond the limitations of the ego.

Another problematic area in the 3rd dimension is alcohol.

Alcohol is a popular and socially acceptable substance that is widely consumed around the world. Many people enjoy drinking alcohol to relax, socialize, or simply have a good time. However, few realize alcohol can lower their vibrations and negatively impact their spiritual, emotional, and physical well-being.

When we talk about vibration, we refer to the energy surrounding and flowing through our bodies. Many internal and external factors influence this energy, including our thoughts, emotions, actions, and environment. Maintaining a high vibration is widely believed to be essential to living a healthy, happy, and fulfilling life.

Alcohol consumption is known to have several adverse effects on our vibration. First and foremost, alcohol is a depressant. It slows down our body's functions, including our heart rate, respiratory rate, and brain activity. This can lead to feelings of drowsiness, lethargy, and even depression.

Also, alcohol has a detrimental effect on our moods and emotions. It is known to alter our brain chemistry, impairing our ability to think clearly, feel positive emotions, and regulate our behavior which can lead to feelings of anger, aggression, anxiety, and depression.

In addition to affecting our emotions and mood, alcohol can also physically affect our bodies. Consuming an excessive amount of alcohol can cause dehydration, which can lead to fatigue, headaches, and muscle weakness. Alcohol can also damage our liver, kidneys, and other organs, leading to long-term health problems and a weaker immune system.

Perhaps most significantly, alcohol consumption can impact our spiritual vibration. Many spiritual traditions believe that we are connected to a higher power and that this connection is necessary for our spiritual growth and well-being. However, alcohol consumption can block this connection, making it more difficult for us to access our higher selves, our intuition, and our connection to the universe.

While alcohol may seem like a harmless way to have fun or unwind, it can have profound negative effects on our vibration. By lowering our mood, impairing our physical and mental health, and blocking our spiritual connection, alcohol can negatively impact our overall well-being. If you choose to consume alcohol, it is essential to do so in moderation and with awareness to avoid the negative effects that come with excessive consumption.

Now that we have uncovered some of the blocks to accession, let's talk about what enhances our soul and helps our vibration to rise. This is my favorite subject.

Forgiveness is a powerful tool that can help you prepare to live in the 5th dimension. The 5th dimension represents a state of consciousness where love, peace, harmony, and unity prevail. It is a higher state of being where you escape the limitations of time, space, and the material world. To reach this state of being, forgiveness plays a crucial role.

Forgiveness is the process of letting go of anger, resentment, blame, and other negative emotions toward oneself or others. It is a conscious choice to release the past and move forward with a new perspective and a renewed sense of peace. Forgiveness is not forgetting or condoning the past but choosing not to dwell on it or let it define your present and future.

To live in the 5th dimension, you must let go of the old patterns and belief systems that no longer serve you. These beliefs and patterns may have been ingrained in you for years and may have caused you deep pain and suffering. Forgiveness helps you break free from these patterns and beliefs, allowing you to experience a new sense of freedom and joy.

Forgiveness also allows you to speak your truth without holding onto anger or resentment. When you forgive, you let go of the need to be right and instead focus on finding a resolution that benefits everyone. This is an essential component of living in the 5th dimension, where compassion and understanding are the primary values.

Moreover, forgiveness allows you to connect with others on a deep level, creating stronger bonds of love, trust, and understanding. In the 5th dimension, relationships are based on mutual respect, empathy, and unconditional love. Forgiveness helps us see beyond our differences and connect with each other at a soul level.

Finally, forgiveness is an essential aspect of self-care. When we forgive ourselves and others, we heal emotional wounds that block our ability to love and be loved. We release the negative energy trapped in our bodies, allowing us to experience greater levels of joy, peace, and clarity.

Forgiveness plays a vital role in helping us prepare to live in the 5th dimension. It liberates us from the limitations of the past, allowing us to embrace a new level of consciousness and connect with the collective energy of love, peace, and harmony. Forgiveness is not just an act of kindness towards others but an essential aspect of our spiritual growth and evolution.

How does forgiveness lead to Self-Love?

Self-love is essential for an individual's overall well-being and happiness. It is the foundation of positive mental health, allowing us to build healthy relationships with others and be content in our skin. Forgiving oneself is an essential aspect of self-love. We often hold onto past mistakes or regrets, which can lead to negative self-talk and a sense of self-doubt. Forgiveness allows us to accept our mistakes and learn from them rather than dwelling on them and continuing to criticize ourselves.

Forgiving oneself also involves letting go of any negative emotions we may hold towards ourselves. When we forgive ourselves, we release ourselves from self-criticism and judgment, which can be incredibly freeing. This helps us cultivate a greater sense of self-compassion and self-love, allowing us to be more forgiving toward others. This is crucial to raise your vibration and to help you ascend to the 5th dimension.

Forgiveness is a critical aspect of self-love. It lets us release negative emotions and move forward into a brighter, happier future. Forgiving oneself involves accepting and learning from our mistakes, allowing us to cultivate more self-compassion and self-love. When we forgive ourselves, we open ourselves up to the possibility of growth and positive change. Embracing forgiveness can help us to become better versions of ourselves and to lead more meaningful, fulfilling lives.

Are you ready for the Fifth Dimension?

One aspect of the fifth dimension is its association with higher consciousness and spiritual awakening. Many spiritual traditions believe that accessing the fifth dimension requires a shift in perception and deepening of one's spiritual practice. It is said to be a realm of expanded awareness where one can connect with higher levels of being and access greater wisdom and insight.

Also, the 5th dimension is considered a place of infinite possibilities and manifestations. In this realm, one can experience a heightened sense of creativity and the ability to manifest one's desires with ease. This may be linked to the idea that thought and intention have a much greater impact on reality in the fifth dimension than in our three-dimensional world.

Finally, the 5th dimension is sometimes associated with the concept of unity consciousness. This refers to a state of being in which one recognizes the interconnectedness of all things and experiences a deep sense of oneness with the universe. By entering this state of consciousness, one can transcend the limitations of the ego and experience a sense of interdependence and interconnectedness with all of creation.

The 5th dimension is a complex and multifaceted concept that touches on many different aspects of human experience. While much about this dimension remains a mystery, scientific research and spiritual traditions suggest that it is a real and important phenomenon with great potential for personal growth and transformation. As we continue to explore the mysteries of the fifth dimension, we may discover new insights into the nature of reality and the meaning of our existence.

Living in the 5th dimension offers a new level of consciousness and understanding. We exist in a state of oneness, where our individuality is transcended, and our interconnectedness is celebrated. Our lives are filled with infinite possibilities as we expand our understanding of what is truly possible.

In conclusion, many people claim to have had experiences in the 5th dimension, which is also known as the astral plane or the spiritual dimension. This dimension is said to exist beyond the physical world and is a realm of higher consciousness where beings have access to higher levels of knowledge and wisdom. Let's explore some of the experiences of a 5th-dimensional existence.

One of the most common experiences people report is feeling "lifted up" or "expanded" beyond their physical body. For me, I feel that my etheric field is greatly expanded, which gives me heightened awareness. Many, including myself, who have experienced this state often describe a sense of peace, love, joy, and a feeling of connectedness to everything around them.

Another experience often reported in the 5th dimension is the ability to communicate in a higher realm. My spirit guides speak to me through meditation or when I spend time in silence. They communicate to provide guidance, comfort or simply to offer a message of love and support. I have also encountered beings from other dimensions or realms, such as extraterrestrial and interdimensional beings. This, too, was during meditation.

I have also experienced a heightened sense of intuition and psychic abilities, including the ability to see and perceive energy, telepathy, clairvoyance, and other forms of extrasensory perception. I could also access information beyond time and space, including past lives.

The 5th dimension offers harmony and unity with all of Mother Earth's creations. This includes a deep understanding of the interconnectedness of all things and a profound respect for the natural world. I now feel a sense of responsibility to help others and work towards improving humanity.

My personal experiences include the following:

The download of messages from my guides.

Timeline Hopping

Astral Travel

Receiving information while practicing quantum healing on my clients

Ability to see energy and work on animals.

Experience and work through a vortex

While the idea of a 5th-dimensional life may seem far-fetched to some, I can tell you that my awakening and transition have been nothing short of miraculous. To live in a consciousness of kindness and joy is amazing. I can experience the love of self and the love of others, including Mother Earth and her occupants. This is a path of great knowledge and wisdom. This is a path to truly be of service to others.

Those of us who were blessed with these amazing gifts have also agreed to share them with others for the benefit of humanity. It is truly a wonderful journey, and I am honored to be able to be here to serve and assist mankind.

***

To contact Nicole:

https://www.facebook.com/nicole.harvick.90/

https://www.instagram.com/nicolesharvick/

(1) Nicole Harvick | LinkedIn

www.nicoleharvick.com

nicoleharvick@gmail.com

My Calendly - Event Types - Calendly

Greg Mester, Jr.

Greg Mester, an Agile Cheerleader, Mentor, Coach, Keynote Speaker and Entrepreneur earning 20 certifications as well as Bachelors and Masters degrees. Greg has Survived and Thrived in Change with 80 job changes. In 1999, Greg started his first business. Then 9/11/2001 and the Fear around the region destroyed it. Almost bankrupt, on the verge of losing his house and walking through movie theater parking lots to find cash for lunch, Greg survived with "Yes's". In 2006, a former project partner, remembering his skills, asked Greg to go to California. That "Yes" led Greg to the Best "Yes" Ever from his wife. He discovered Agile and Scrum, which he used to save Million Dollar programs and doubled his salary with "Yes's" to job changes in a few years. In a 2018 interview, a VP wanted a more well-known Agile Leader. #5amMesterScrum was born in 2019 to create Future "Yes's". Greg has grown 13,000+ connections on LinkedIn and #5amMesterScrum to 12,000 subscribers and 14 million views on YouTube, a 2023 #4 Ranked Podcast for Agile Coaching by Feedspot and Greg has spoken around the world. He has survived and thrived in change during his lifetime; now restarting his business alongside #5amMesterScrum with the Mission of Getting People Home to Family & Friends, Growing Business Value, while Balancing Work & Life with Less Stress & More Fun.

You Can Thrive in a Lifetime of Change

By Greg Mester, Jr.

Learning About No's from Others and How to Make Them Yes's

As an average student, I have always had to fight through barriers and assumed paths in high school and college. In High School, I wanted to take AP Chemistry, but I was not an honors student. Turning the "No" took convincing the chemistry teacher and I got a "Yes". My Goal was not straight A's, but to push myself into more difficult learning experiences and to see what the "Smart" students were learning. My level of high school math set me back in Engineering. I was placed in a lower-level trig class instead of calculus which was needed 1st semester to graduate in four years. I asked, "was there a rule that said I could not take both trig and calculus at the same time?" and of course it was "No." Turning that "No" into "Yes" meant me taking both classes at the same time.

My 1990 graduation was in time for one of the worst hiring rates in 10 years. I have an entire notebook of "No's" on engineering applications and said "Yes" 5 or 6 different jobs to make ends meet. One of those "Yes" jobs turned out to be a multi-level marketing scheme selling perfume door-to-door. I received 100 "No's" before the first "Yes". Cold Calling or door-to-door is the best way to develop a tough skin for "No's" and to keep looking for that one "Yes".

- You or your Team must do the Work for the "Yes" and not depend on others! (So Grant Cardone)

My life in the federal service and corporate world was all about finding ways for people to say "Yes" to me and learning from every "No". I always asked for things initially because I figured I had nothing to lose from a "No". The clerks were the only ones with computers, so when they upgraded their computers, I asked for one of the old P/S2's. "Yes" they said. Leveraging the "Yes", I increased my productivity by 5X. Writing a "coffee" program that ran while I got coffee to create a list of potential high value proposal work to choose from, a list of vendors to satisfy the same proposal and I would have multiple proposals soon enough. That "coffee" program would also provide the locations of all my proposals in review at any Navy engineering command. As soon as the package was on an engineer's desk, they would receive a phone call from me. I developed a good working relationship with all the commands because I would reach out for a "Yes" and continuously improve my proposals for more "Yes's".

- Leverage a "Yes" to make even more "Yes's"

During one project, I presented to the Under Secretary of the Navy. I learned how to get a "Yes" for funding approval by making the effort look tiny compared to the big picture. A $10M program disappeared when looking at the entire Billion-dollar Navy engine program and smaller than our command's $17B budget. Making it easy for them to say "Yes" and Success. This is where I first learned about Real Money. Millions compared to Billions is Nothing, in the big scheme of business or life.

While in California, we won $35M+ for an Army upgrade program. The problem it created was too much money in one bucket, other high-value programs wanted a cut. Every time the program manager visited Detroit; less money was in our budget. I had to make this "Yes" into a better "Yes", so we could keep more funds. The next funding round, I created six proposals that totaled $25M+. Since the projects were smaller, there was no more reaching into the buckets. I got what we needed by keeping "Yes's" small.

- Keeping it Simple and Small with an Understanding of Customer Capabilities make "Yes" possible.

Years later, I was working on a product competing against a well-known company and its live-streaming program. We wanted to be 1st in the market. The way the teams were laid out (what I call Scrum-a-Fall), it would take us years to finish. Pulling the team together in a true co-located Agile Team, with no communication barriers, resulted in getting it Done and Delivered it on Time! My director asked, "How did you do it?" My answer was "We got them all in a room working together as a team and not six different teams".

We broke the mold. Later, an Executive frowned on the approach and said, "We would never do that again". Every project done in the old way was basically a month to 6-months late. Nothing was worth a lifetime of getting yelled at for projects being late. That "No" was the sign to move on.

- Some "No's" are code words for Time to Move on to Opportunities that say "Yes"!

Opportunities to Say "Yes" for Yourself

So many people even today, some 30 years since I graduated from college, will never leave their current corporate position, no matter how much they complain. They don't know how to say "Yes" for themselves and take advantage of the opportunities.

In my early federal service days, they offered to pay for three college classes a year. I took advantage even though it did not pay for a full year of my master's in business management. I got paid about $27K per year with $200 bonuses. I treated that college reimbursement like a huge bonus that would pay for years to come. One co-worker approached me and asked, "What I did do to deserve the benefit?". I responded, "They were offering it, and I was taking it". It so easily could have been a "No" based on others' opinions or the fact that I had to find the money for another 2 classes a year, rather I found a way to say "Yes" for myself. I'm still benefiting from that "Yes" 33 years later!

But this does not happen today, right? Well hold your hat. I was an agile coach for one company and persuaded the CIO to offer the Teams free Scrum training. The product owners refused to take the class even though the company was paying for their time and the class. They were quote, "too busy, and they knew all they needed". Excuses for "No". In a little over a year, that company was acquired, and IT was laid off. I felt terrible for those Product Owners who said "No". Everyone who said "Yes" had certifications for their resumes. There are things in the corporate world that NONE of us can control.

- You should Never Pass Up Free or Discounted Training, Find a Way to say "Yes" (so Alex Hormozi)

A few years into federal service there was an internship advertisement to work in DC on the F/A-18E/F program. I could have said "No" because there were hundreds of people that could apply. Maybe my coworkers were waiting for others lead or everyone was too busy? I could have said "No" as I was in the middle of my master's program and twice a week, I had to commute 5 hours round trip from DC to Philly and back. I could have said "No", but I applied, and I got a "Yes". That "Yes" allowed me to participate in 1st Flight planning and coordinating the $8 Billion Low-Rate Initial Production Specification (again, a lesson in the relative size of money). It was a GREAT experience that I will remember forever because I made it a "Yes".

- Do what YOU can to fit a "Yes" in, even if tough. Think Long-Term and even Fun.

A higher-level Navy command called one day asking, "If we wanted $700K for our project." With "No" in mind, my junior engineer was like, "But we don't know what to do with it?" I responded, "Yes, take it and we would figure it out later. But get the money before they give it to someone else." That "Yes" opened the door to future presentation to the Under Secretary of the Navy.

- Say "Yes" to the Unknown Opportunities and you can figure it out later.

Many new contract jobs are 6 months to permanent and so many people are looking for that perfect job, so they say "No". For those with no experience, it can be a perfect opportunity to say "Yes". Develop a budget, so you can calculate your minimum rate to say "Yes". This budget process is just as applicable to career people in a company as contractors / consultants. The job might not be perfect, but it provides income and, best of all, experience for later "Yes's".

- Preparing your budget numbers is critical to saying "Yes" to new jobs or accepting new clients.

Two things that everyone should do to empower yourselves to say "Yes":

  (1) Buy your Own Life Insurance
  (2) Quote Health Insurance and buy your Own.

It is incredible how these two insurances prevent people from saying "Yes" to changing positions or finding new opportunities. Plus, one never knows when benefits, that others control, could just disappear. Today, there is Healthcare.gov and it is easy to determine how good your insurance coverage really is.

- Say "Yes" to Freedom by Owning Your Own Insurance Policies (So Bob Proctor)

Transforming Mindset into Results

Breaking the Fear barrier as Les Brown speaks of was preventing me from saying "Yes" and pursuing my own business once again for round two. I had to retrain my brain, to say "Yes". I made other businesses millions of dollars and why I could not do it for myself? On January 20, 2021, Todd L. Bauerle, contacted me via LinkedIn and asked me what was stopping me from living my dream. The answer was a cushy-paying job and my FEAR mindset. I said call me back in 6 months (contract cycle). That May, I had a mindset conflict with what I was doing. Here is what I wrote Todd in an email on May 18, 2021:

> Todd, I caught your show today. It was not necessarily the show, but I think I'm ready to move forward. So how much does it cost and how does it work? Sincerely, Greg Mester

That "Yes" opened the door for massive mindset changes as I found Bob Proctor through the "Thinking Into Results" TIR program that Todd coached. I consumed Mindset and growth books, watched videos, and listened to podcasts and still do today.

Books: Napoleon Hill, "Think and Grow Rich"; Bob Proctor, "You Were Born Rich"; Russell H Conwell, "Acres of Diamonds" (a big Philadelphia Connection); Grant Cardone, "The 10X Rule" just to mention a few in addition to works by Les Brown, Jim Britt and Jim Lutes.

Three things were consistent from this consuming of knowledge from Millionaires and Billionaires:

1) Every day, Be Thankful and Write Goals.
2) Get a Coach or Mentor.
3) Join Mastermind Groups.

Thank You's and Goals in a Daily Habit:

I write down five areas of thought in a notebook daily. I do this before emails or social media, so I control my day and don't let others control it. "Atomic Habits" by James Clear is so good on establishing good habits. My five areas:

1) 10 Things I'm Thankful for (see Rhonda Byrne's book "The Magic" and try her 28-day program – All of it! – I practice the Magic Rock exercise nightly – It's a no brainer.)
2) Two Versions of my Goals: Lifetime Super Goals and Short-6-month to Year
    a. I write in a simple key word list format for both versions in case time is short.
    b. I write in long-form my Goals again to help me visualize them in my mind. Something I learned in "Thinking Into Results".
3) I write down what things I'm NOT Doing as a reminder to myself.
4) I write down due dates for the next few weeks. I learned from Jim Lutes and Jim Britt that dates motivate and hold us accountable. So true!
5) Lastly, I write down my day's To Do Items. Using the other four areas to prioritize, so I can say "Yes".

Coaches and Mentors:

As a coach, I believe coaches who say "No" to being coached or mentored are more about "No's" than "Yes's". How can we ask people to say "Yes" to coaching, if we don't say "Yes" to coaching ourselves?

"Yes" to agile coaches included a 6-month Expert Agile program to stretch my coaching skills and one coach taught me how to get certified to teach agile classes.

That "Yes" to "Thinking Into Results" resulted in coaching, mentoring and Masterminding to change my mindset for "Yes." Honestly, it took me a year to say "Yes" and punch through that Fear barrier. Having a coach to challenge me on business and personal goal fronts was great and just what I needed to say "Yes". I needed something to fight off all the negativity, doubt, fear, and worry from years of corporate programming, as Jim Britt likes to say.

I said "Yes" to a few coaches for Marketing to learn working frameworks, so I didn't have to build from scratch (a theme from all the Billionaires).

My latest "Yes" came in the form of this book, which resulted in my latest mentors Jim Lutes and Jim Britt for my public speaking, how to use speaking to grow my business, marketing and sales. Plus, a bonus of mindset coaching all around. Jack Pot!

On an Add Value to Entrepreneurs podcast episode, they recommend three coaches, two mentors and one Mastermind. The coaches cover Accountability, Business and Mindset. The mentors are all about the "Yes's" for future you, not where you are now.

Key to a good coaching experience is to develop a goal within the first couple of sessions of what you want to achieve. I have tried coaching the "What would you like to talk about today approach?", and it fails after just a few sessions. Without goals, we just wander aimlessly and might not see a benefit for future "Yes's"?

- Say "Yes" to Coaches, Mentors and Mastermind and work on Your Goals together.

Join a Mastermind!

To be honest, I find something magical about Mastermind groups. It is not necessarily the answers given or received. The group for me, opens my mind to change and new "Yes's", both external and from within.

Like coaching, having goals is critical to being successful with a Mastermind. I consumed Mastermind books: Tobe Brockner, "Mastermind Group Blueprint"; Cicely Maxwell, "How to create a Mastermind Group" plus the books mentioned before and not mentioned.

I include Scrum and Personal Objectives and Key Results (OKR's) in my Mastermind groups for my coaching programs. You might ask, "Why?" Well, there is usually a small mention in a few books about ACCOUNTABILITY. Accountability is a key for Mastermind

Success. I witnessed many mastermind people saying "No" by not coming prepared to share. They need structure to support "Yes".

My solution for "Yes" was to make things small. Each Mastermind time-box is a 3-month quarter with four 3-week timeboxes. Remember smaller makes it easier to say "Yes". At the beginning of each quarter, we establish personal OKRs. Then, for every 3-week Sprint, we make small list of to work towards our goals (Sprint Planning). Once a week, we meet virtually to share our successes and blockers. The mastermind tries to help work out the blockers "No's" and inspire "Yes's". Mastermind members present what they produced at the end of each Sprint and Quarter (Sprint Review). And we repeat for the next "Yes".

- Adding Personal OKRs and Sprint Events is Key to Accountability in a Mastermind

One last item, important in any Mastermind or any Team, is a set of team norms that everyone agrees to. Learned from TIR, this is the most important:

> "I FORGIVE - I forgive myself for mistakes I have made. I also forgive others who have hurt me in the past, so I can move into the future with a clean slate."

Without forgiveness, we can never say "Yes" to the future, and we will be stuck in the past with "No". Face it, we ALL Make Mistakes. Making mistakes key to saying "Yes" to exponential growth; sometimes, those mistakes hurt ourselves and others and can create "No's".

- To Forgive is to create a possible "Yes's" for everyone.

Work on those "Yes's" from Others, allow Yourself to say "Yes" for your own benefit and change your Mindset to not Fear Change, but know you can Survive and Thrive in a continuous life of Change. "Yes"!

***

To Contact Greg:

Greg Mester, President of Idea Communication Networks, Incorporated for Corporate Coaching

Website: https://www.IdeaCommNets.com

Email: connect@ideacommnets.com

Greg Mester, Co-Host #5amMesterScrum for agile speaking, coaching, masterminding or wanting to join us on a show

Website & Blog: https://www.5amMesterScrum.com

Email: connect@5amMesterScrum.com

@5amMesterScrum for Youtube, Facebook, Instagram, X (old twitter) and TikTok

Greg Mester LinkedIn: https://www.linkedin.com/in/gregmester/

5amMesterScrum LinkedIn: https://www.linkedin.com/company/5ammesterscrum/

Podcasts: Search in your favorite podcast app for 5amMesterScrum and you should find us

Stacie Shifflett

Founder & CEO of Modern Consciousness®, LLC

Entrepreneur | Modern Consciousness Coach® | International Best-Selling Author

Stacie Shifflett, founder of Modern Consciousness®, is a catalyst for personal transformation. With a diverse background in multiple industries, she has become a sought-after expert in empowering individuals to reclaim joy and peace of mind.

In 2012, a life-changing event propelled Stacie on a quest to better understand herself and the human condition in general. Her immersive exploration with experts in diverse fields of study ignited a deep desire to guide others toward embracing their unique brilliance and finding their joy.

As CEO of Modern Consciousness®, Stacie channels her insights to help individuals raise awareness of unconscious patterns from the past. By shifting these patterns intentionally, she enables clients to transform their lives from frustration to internal peace and joy. Stacie firmly believes that embracing Modern Consciousness® is the secret sauce to a life well-lived.

Stacie's credentials speak to her dedication and expertise. She is a multi-time international bestselling author, a Modern Consciousness Coach®, a certified ThetaHealer®, a Free-mE® Emotional Freedom Technique (EFT) Practitioner, and a Master Practitioner of Neurolinguistic Programming. Her expertise extends to being a Professional Neuro-Shine Technology Coach™ and a Certified High-Performance Coach™.

Through her visionary leadership at Modern Consciousness®, she empowers individuals worldwide to embrace their innate brilliance and experience authentic joy and peace.

Difficult Women: Awaken Your Extraordinary and Embrace the Power of Transformation

By Stacie Shifflett

"Really? This is where you want to take this conversation?"

After nine months of pushing the proverbial rock uphill, I sat in a private office at a large conference table. Just the three of us. Myself, of course, the partner I had invited into the deal to help me accomplish this, and the man hired by the investment company to fill the role of CEO whom we had just met.

In the days prior to this meeting, my associate and I had closed on the acquisition of a tech company worth tens of millions of dollars. It was quite a feat as we did this without investing a penny. We had been told countless times that what we wanted to do as 'cashless investors' (which is what the business broker called us) was impossible. Despite the challenges, we persevered and achieved our goal. As part of the deal, we also had employment contracts that explicitly outlined our roles in the company, specified our salaries, and designated the percentage of the company we now owned as a 'finder's fee.' Mine included. Yet here we were in a meeting with the new CEO, enthusiastically unveiling the organizational chart he put together, and guess what? My name wasn't on it.

"Sooooo….I don't see my name anywhere on this chart?" I asked.

"No," he said and paused. Then, with a raised eyebrow and a chuckle, he said, "I really don't know what to do with you."

"You don't?" I questioned, my voice firm as I leaned into the conversation. "Well let me remind you of two things. First, you wouldn't be here if it wasn't for me because this whole thing was my idea. I made this happen, not you. Secondly, and even more importantly, I have an employment contract with the investment firm that just purchased this company which clearly delineates my position on that org chart of yours." Then I walked out.

My partner on the deal – who I had recruited to join me on my quest to acquire this company as he had contacts in the merger and acquisition world and an MBA (I had neither) – caught up with me in front of the elevator.

"Hey…slow down…where are you going?" he asked.

"Where does it look like I'm going? I'm leaving."

"You can't do that! Come back in and we'll work this out. Plus, you can't talk to him that way. He's our new boss."

"Well, yes, I can talk to him any way I choose, actually," I said, and then, "I didn't hear you speak up and say anything in my defense. How would you feel if he left YOU off the org chart?"

But, of course, he didn't omit him. He omitted *me b*ecause he didn't know what to do with me. He clarified why a bit later.

You see, my partner had the credentials that I lacked. He attended an Ivy League school and had an impressive MBA. On the other hand, I took a different path. I started working at the age of 16 as a waitress in a family restaurant. You know the kind. They serve breakfast all day, the coffee's always on, and the fried chicken dinner is the fav of the after-church Sunday crowd.

From there, while I attended George Mason University for nearly three years pursuing a degree in Business Administration, I supported myself by working as a cocktail waitress and bartender. I was earning decent money, so I questioned the necessity of completing my degree. Why couldn't I have a career in the restaurant business? I've always been one to challenge the norms and think outside the box, so I quit.

One time, during my years in the hospitality industry, I walked into a bar that I was familiar with, took a seat, ordered a drink, and asked to speak to the owner. When he appeared, I boldly suggested that he needed to hire me, and when he asked why, I confidently replied, "Because I can substantially increase your revenue. I've studied your drink prices, observed your clientele as a customer, and recognized the untapped potential in this business. You're leaving money on the table." He hired me on the spot, and we successfully increased the bar's revenue together.

The Change[20]

After getting married in 1983, I transitioned to an office job so I would not work nights and weekends. I figured office hours would be more conducive to married life. I found a job doing basic bookkeeping and typing for a small woman-owned government contractor. Within a year or so of taking that entry-level position, I nearly single-handedly rolled out the first IBM desktop computers to the entire U.S. Department of Health and Human Services. The tech guys put them together. I created and delivered all of the training and user support. I like to say that I took to the tech industry like a duck to water.

I thrived in that environment effortlessly. I was personally motivated, had a natural aptitude for learning, and unwavering determination. My mindset was open and adaptable, and I grasped concepts quickly. I exuded confidence, was always hungry for knowledge, and was driven to expand my skills. Moreover, my intelligence served as a valuable asset, enhancing my ability to excel at whatever I chose to do. My employer and her clients loved me.

In the early nineties, I began a help desk position at a company that automated federal government procurement processes. It was fundamental automation back then. Long story short, from there, I proceeded to work my way up to being a highly regarded and sought-after Subject Matter Expert in the field of federal acquisition and procurement. I didn't look for work. Employers sought me based on my reputation in this niche industry.

Yet, despite my qualifications and successful career, I found myself fully immersed in an unexpected situation. After orchestrating the acquisition of a company whose entire market was in my field of expertise, I was left off the org chart. Because he didn't know what to do with an unconventional woman, excuse me?

And if that wasn't enough, my partner told me I was being the difficult one in this scenario and that I needed to yield to this man even though he was clearly violating the terms of my employment contract. He knew what the contract said.

Such is the reality of being labeled a 'difficult' woman. Some individuals struggle to comprehend our unique essence, unsure how to navigate our presence. Others eagerly embrace our remarkable qualities, recognizing that they can rely on us to deliver. They also appreciate our unwavering loyalty. In return, we hold the expectation that they reciprocate the same level of commitment and dedication toward us.

As I reflect now on my journey through life, I can't help but notice the recurring theme of being labeled difficult. The term my family used frequently when I didn't follow the 'rules' was 'stubborn.' For example, I was a bartender, and my parents were teetotalers. I was coloring outside the lines of what they thought and what they thought society thought was a respectable profession. But they supported me anyway.

My ex-husband called me difficult because I desired to spend time with him, and, well, he didn't have time for that. He was building a business, and, as he put it, his job was to support our family financially. Since he was doing that and fulfilling his role, I needed to leave him alone and figure out how to entertain myself. So, I did. I built a career, raised a family, made millions, and traveled with friends.

But what I really notice, especially working with women in my coaching practice, is that this label is not unique to my own experiences. It's a rather pervasive cultural perception. In both personal and professional spheres, women who are assertive, ambitious, outspoken, willing to stand up for themselves, and who challenge societal norms are often deemed 'difficult.' But are we? What is the true essence of a 'difficult' woman?

I'm huge on definitions. I believe that aligning them is essential to any conversation. So let me tell you that by 'difficult' woman, I do not mean bossy, controlling, manipulative, unreasonable, belligerent, emotionally immature, moody, tactless, or malicious. Those aren't admirable traits in anybody, regardless of gender. What I do mean is women who authentically demonstrate assertiveness, determination, courage, resilience, self-reliance, self-assuredness, creativity, and empowerment with grace, emotional intelligence, and effective and empathetic communication. These characteristics are impressive for anyone, man or woman.

I recently had an interesting conversation with a successful woman who stated that she viewed her drive for achievement as a weakness, interfering with her ability to create a truly fulfilling life. She believed that her pursuit of accomplishments reduced her capacity to genuinely appreciate the richness that all of life has to offer. She also believed that being a high achiever interfered with her ability to connect with her intuition and Spirit.

What was getting in her way of deep fulfillment? Her goals had shifted without her realization, as had her values.

You see, these things change over time, and we are often not consciously aware of that internal shift. Why? Because we've drifted into allowing the activities of our lives to create the momentum that pushes us forward in our world. We stopped being intentional about them. Sure, we made choices when we were younger, such as what career to pursue, getting married, or starting a family. Then, as we continue to add things to our already busy lives, generally with the best intentions, we succumb to doing our best to keep up with what's already in motion. Basically, this woman was ready to step out of Automaton, which is the first aspect of my theory of Modern Consciousness® and into the next, the Awakening Soul.

Awakening Souls begin a journey to gain knowledge and a deeper understanding of themselves, their situations, and those around them. They begin to acknowledge that there might be other possibilities in life. They have an inner knowing that life can be better. They even start to wonder what they are contributing to the situation and what keeps them bound to their current circumstance even though they aren't happy.

Awakening Souls are the seekers of knowledge and answers. As their knowledge increases, generally due to exposure to others who have already made this journey, they adapt and align to new teachings and rewire their old limiting beliefs. They begin to heal, leading them to a more satisfying inner life, which, of course, also begins to reflect in their outer life. This aspect of Modern Consciousness® can be rough as emotions that have been 'stuffed' or ignored for what is sometimes a long period of time (since childhood even) surface for release and healing. Many people in this stage also seek a spiritual path, not in terms of religion per se, but in terms of our connection to Source and others. They may adopt practices such as meditation or seek healing from those trained in energetic modalities. It's a period of learning and experimentation. As they continue to learn and grow and gain competence in areas such as emotional regulation and self-awareness - from a place of curiosity rather than self-judgment, a significant distinction there – they step into what I call an Illuminated Adept.

Someone who is adept at something is trained and skilled in that area. Within Modern Consciousness®, the Illuminated Adept builds upon what they learned as an Awakening Soul. They continue to seek, gain, and integrate knowledge into their lives, and, as a result, they begin to witness profound positive changes within themselves, including experiencing longer and more frequent periods of inner peace, joy, and contentment. As people gain mastery in more areas of life, such as focusing on the present, accepting things outside of their control with grace, and opening themselves to forgiveness, gratitude, and appreciation, they step into the role of inspiring others.

This brings me to the fourth aspect of Modern Consciousness®, the Transformer. Transformers have radically changed their lives and the lives of those in their orbit. They have entered a realm in which they engage with the world in such a way as to contribute positively to humanity and the planet *consistently*. They have generally overcome fear and live primarily from a place of love.

These aspects of Modern Consciousness® aren't linear; we flow organically between them. Why? Because there is always more to learn, and life never tires of helping us level up. For example, an Illuminated Adept might slip back into the Automaton stage if they find themselves drowning in their business activities or experiencing a life-changing event that shifts their purpose, and they feel lost. These are my favorite clients as they have a reservoir of knowledge and skills they can tap into even if they are currently on unsteady ground. They have already begun their personal evolution. They aren't in crisis, but they desire assistance maneuvering their current situation and incorporating what they've learned into their lives meaningfully and practically. And, of course, these new experiences aid them in expanding their knowledge even further.

Can you discern what aspect (or aspects) of Modern Consciousness® you are currently living? And, even more importantly, have you awakened your extraordinary?

I chose the title for my chapter in this book as it encapsulates my personal journey. The implosion of my 28-year marriage was the catalyst that set me on an intentional transformational path, one that has spanned more than a decade now. As I navigated this personal challenge, my life experiences, knowledge, and an undeniable spiritual connection guided me to a place I never thought possible. Today, I firmly believe that true transformation begins within, and my life's purpose has evolved into something grander than just a personal journey. It led me to start my current business and create 'Elevate Your Life®' – my life transformational program grounded in the theory of Modern Consciousness®.

I desire to create profound change in the world, one person at a time. As Margaret Mead once wisely said, "never believe that a few caring people can't change the world" – and that's precisely what I aim to accomplish. How? By guiding individuals through their transformation process, which, in turn, ripples outward with the energetic potential to influence everyone in their orbit positively. From their personal relationships to their businesses and organizations, from their communities to society at large.

The goal of my comprehensive program, 'Elevate Your Life®,' is to put you directly on the path of intentionally creating the life you want to live by increasing your clarity about the life you are currently living, defining your aspirations for the life you want to be living, and developing a practical strategy that moves you in the direction of your aspirations. It's all about reclaiming your power, genius, and joy rather than sitting in a place of indecision and taking no action.

Elevate Your Life® offers a powerful and transformative journey toward intentional living and self-empowerment. The Modern Consciousness® Ascension Formula, with its five essential steps, serves as the roadmap to guide individuals from their current reality to the life they aspire to lead.

In Step 1, the Assessment, we set the foundation by evaluating your current life and gaining a clear understanding of where you are today. This step is akin to setting the starting point on your GPS, which is vital for charting your path to your desired future. Surprisingly, many of us diligently evaluate various aspects of our lives, from health to finances, but rarely take a comprehensive look at our lives as a whole. Elevate Your Life® addresses this by clarifying what you are currently experiencing in all areas of your life.

Next, in Step 2, we define your Aspirations, illuminating the destinations you wish to reach in all aspects of your life. This module also delves into your core values and character strengths, reinforcing the authenticity and depth of your aspirations.

As the magic unfolds in Step 3, Architecting the Bridge, we explore and acknowledge the gaps between your current reality and your desired future. Uncovering recurring themes empowers you to identify and address underlying patterns that may manifest differently in various areas of your life. This deeper awareness accelerates positive change and paves the way for transformation.

Step 4, Activation propels you forward with practical and actionable steps. These meaningful actions generate steady progress, reinforcing your commitment and inspiring you to continue toward your ultimate goal.

Finally, Step 5, Alignment, ensures that the transformative changes you've cultivated are integral to your daily life. This is where we align your habitual thoughts, behaviors, activities, and emotions with your aspirations, which is essential to achieving success.

Elevate Your Life® goes beyond fleeting or temporary changes you cannot sustain. It empowers you to embody lasting transformation consciously and intentionally. The program demands active participation and dedication, as you hold the key to your life's direction. Through compassionate guidance and non-judgmental support, we embark on an intensive journey of self-discovery and growth. We bring your frustrations, desires, and aspirations into your conscious awareness, and together, we create the magic that transforms your life.

In the end, Elevate Your Life® is a testament to your sovereignty and autonomy, allowing you to shape your destiny and awaken your extraordinary potential. Like the mighty oak already resides in the acorn, the magic to your desired future already lies within you, ready to be unlocked and harnessed on this extraordinary journey of transformation. If you're ready to unleash your brilliance, genius, and joy, I invite you to connect with me.

***

To contact Stacie:

Website: www.ModernConsciousness.com

Facebook: https://www.facebook.com/ModernConsciousness/

Instagram: https://www.instagram.com/modernconsciousness/

LinkedIn: https://www.linkedin.com/in/stacie-shifflett-7b5a8922/

You may contact Ms. Shifflett at Empower@Aware.Life

Shantae Bridges

Shantae Bridges, renowned as the FurBabyLady, boasts a remarkable career as a Canine Care Specialist spanning over a decade. During this time, she has expertly cared for more than 300 dogs nationwide and achieved notable six-figure success.

In 2022, Shantae founded the Elevated Entrepreneur Club, rapidly becoming an essential resource for entrepreneurs seeking brand elevation. Her visionary leadership extends to groundbreaking initiatives such as a global canine app and the world's first luxurious dog boarding facilities.

Shantae's dedication goes beyond business; her true passion lies in improving the lives of dogs and their owners. Her unwavering commitment to this cause has positioned her as an influential leader in the canine care industry.

From Solitude to Triumph

The Entrepreneur's Path of Delegation, Collaboration, and Mentorship

By Shantae Bridges, aka FurBabyLady

During my initial five years as an entrepreneur in the natural hair and skincare industry, I wore all the hats in my one-person show. From product creation to sales, I handled it all. While my passion was the driving force behind my endeavor, the overwhelming tasks drained my time and energy. In hindsight, I realize that delegation was the missing piece that could have saved me time and accelerated my business. These early years were filled with valuable lessons that would shape my entrepreneurial journey.

In those formative years, I had a profound realization. Although my natural hair and skincare business was successful, it didn't align with my true passion. As it grew, I felt a growing disconnect. My heart was somewhere else.

The success and experience I gained in the early years afforded me the freedom to pivot and follow my true calling. I found myself irresistibly drawn to providing premium canine services on a national scale. This shift from skincare to canines was both a strategic business decision and a profound realization of where my true passion lay.

The transition from natural hair and skincare to the canine industry marked an exhilarating new chapter in my entrepreneurial journey. This journey began with the creation of a nationwide dog walking app, revolutionizing the way premium canine services were provided.

The dog walking app represented a significant departure from my previous business, a bold leap into uncharted territory where my passion for canines met my entrepreneurial spirit. Despite the challenges, my unwavering dedication to the cause and deep passion for canines drove me forward.

Over time, the app gained popularity, simplifying the lives of dog owners and creating job opportunities for professional dog walkers. The success of the app underscored the transformative power of pursuing one's true passion, benefiting both individuals and their beloved pets.

The transition wasn't just a change of business; it transformed my entire entrepreneurial journey. It was a journey of self-discovery, a realization that my heart's true calling lay in serving the needs of canines and their owners. The experience and knowledge I gained from my earlier business provided a solid foundation for my foray into the canine industry.

My initial years as a solo entrepreneur in natural hair and skincare taught me the importance of passion and perseverance. They also underscored the significance of delegation, a crucial missing piece in my early days. These years shaped my understanding of entrepreneurship and ultimately led me to my true passion in the world of premium canine services. The creation of the nationwide dog walking app marked a pivotal moment in my journey, showcasing the transformative power of pursuing one's true passion. This chapter in my entrepreneurial story emphasizes the importance of listening to one's heart and having the courage to embrace change when it leads to a more fulfilling and purpose-driven path.

In the early days of my entrepreneurial journey, I was faced with a profound and transformative experience. The weight of an entire venture rested solely on my shoulders, and I found myself responsible for the care and well-being of over 300 dogs scattered across the nation. This endeavor was unlike any other I had undertaken before, and it demanded unwavering dedication and a relentless commitment. Yet, beyond the realm of business, it became something far more significant—a labor of love that would kindle a profound and enduring passion for canines.

The sheer scale of this responsibility was overwhelming. Each day presented a new set of challenges, from coordinating schedules for dog walkers to ensuring the proper nutrition and addressing the individual needs of each dog. It was a demanding, albeit incredibly fulfilling, endeavor. The dogs I cared for varied in size, breed, and temperament, but they all shared one thing in common—a deep need for love, care, and attention.

The most remarkable aspect of this journey was the deep and lasting connections I formed with these wonderful four-legged companions. Every day, I was greeted with wagging tails, joyful barks, and the trusting glances of these dogs. The trust they placed in me was a daily reminder of the immense responsibility I had taken on, and it motivated me to provide the best care possible.

My journey in the canine industry wasn't merely a career pivot; it was a reflection of my unwavering commitment to excellence in premium canine care. This transition marked a pivotal turning point in my professional life, one that I could never have foreseen in my early years as an entrepreneur. It became a testament to my unwavering determination to follow my true passion, a passion that had been ignited by the deep and meaningful connections I had formed with these animals.

Caring for these dogs required a level of dedication and attention to detail that went far beyond what I had experienced in my previous entrepreneurial venture. It was not just about providing a service; it was about becoming an integral part of their lives, ensuring their well-being, and creating an environment where they could truly thrive. It was a journey that was about building trust, not only with the dogs but also with their owners who entrusted us with the care of their beloved pets.

As I immersed myself in the world of canine care, I was driven to pursue continuous learning and improvement. I sought out extensive training and education in dog behavior, nutrition, and health. I assembled a team of dedicated professionals who shared my passion and commitment to providing top-notch care for our furry clients.

The bond I formed with these dogs was truly special. It was about creating a space where their unique personalities could shine, addressing their individual needs, and ensuring their overall happiness and well-being. It wasn't just about providing a service; it was about enriching their lives and fostering a sense of belonging.

In the canine industry, every day presented an opportunity to make a profound and positive impact on the lives of these dogs and their owners. I witnessed the transformation of anxious, shy, or troubled dogs into happy, well-adjusted companions. It filled me with a sense of purpose and fulfillment that went beyond the realms of business. It was about making a meaningful difference in the lives of these animals and their devoted owners.

This chapter in my entrepreneurial story was more than just a business endeavor; it was a profound life-changing experience. It was a testament to the power of passion, dedication, and a deep commitment to making a difference in the lives of animals. It was a journey that expanded my horizons, pushed my limits, and enriched my life in ways I could never have imagined.

My transition from a solo entrepreneur in natural hair and skincare to a pioneer in the premium canine care industry was not just a change of business; it was a transformation of my entire life. It was a journey of passion, dedication, and a commitment to excellence in the care of these beloved animals. My work in the canine industry was a testament to the profound impact that following one's true passion can have, not only on one's career but on the lives of others – in this case, the lives of hundreds of loyal and loving canine companions and their devoted owners.

This transition was a defining moment in my entrepreneurial journey. It went beyond merely changing industries; it was a profound shift in my life's purpose and the embodiment of my deep love for canines. I had transitioned from the world of natural hair and skincare to a new realm where I was dedicated to nurturing and caring for man's best friend.

As FurBabyLady K-9 Care continued to evolve and thrive, I began to recognize the immense potential in creating a global community of pet experts. It was more than just building a brand; it was about uniting passionate individuals from diverse corners of the world, all connected by their shared love for canines. This dynamic team would not only bring unparalleled expertise to the table but also infuse fresh perspectives into the ever-evolving canine industry.

My mission was crystal clear: to empower others to stand out in this vibrant landscape. Together, we embarked on a journey of growth, collaboration, and innovation, redefining what it meant to provide premium canine services. We were armed with diverse skill sets and experiences, perfectly poised to make a lasting impact on the industry. Our aim was to set new standards for excellence, and our shared love for dogs served as the driving force behind our efforts.

In parallel with community building, I saw an opportunity to launch a groundbreaking global dog walking app. This innovative platform aimed to revolutionize how canine care was accessed and delivered on an international scale. It went beyond mere convenience; it was about creating a seamless, premium experience for dogs and their owners worldwide, all under the banner of FurBabyLady K-9 Care.

This expansion of our services was not just a business decision; it was a reflection of our commitment to providing the best care for our canine companions. The global dog walking app would not only make the lives of dog owners easier but would also provide meaningful job opportunities for passionate dog lovers who wanted to become professional dog walkers.

The process of building a global community of pet experts was an exciting and challenging endeavor. We scoured the globe to find individuals who shared our passion and values, who were committed to the well-being of dogs and who could bring unique skills to the table. This community became a hub of knowledge and expertise, enabling us to provide top-tier services, from training and grooming to health and nutrition.

Our united front in the canine industry allowed us to be at the forefront of innovation. We constantly sought ways to improve our services, embracing the latest technology and insights. The diverse perspectives within our team were a source of inspiration, leading to the development of new approaches and solutions to common canine care challenges.

The launch of the global dog walking app was a significant milestone in our journey. It was not just a business venture; it was a mission to make the lives of dog owners and their pets more enjoyable. The app was designed to provide easy access to trusted dog walkers, ensuring that dogs received the care and exercise they needed while their owners had peace of mind.

The transition from natural hair and skincare to the world of premium canine services marked a profound shift in my life and entrepreneurial journey. It led to the creation of FurBabyLady K-9 Care, a platform dedicated to nurturing and caring for dogs and building a global community of passionate pet experts. This chapter in my story is a testament to the power of following one's true passion and embracing innovation to make a meaningful impact on the lives of dogs and their owners worldwide. The global dog walking app and our community-building efforts are more than just business initiatives; they are a reflection of our unwavering commitment to excellence in the world of canine care.

The expansion of FurBabyLady K-9 Care into the world of luxury dog boarding marked an extraordinary phase in our entrepreneurial journey. It was a chapter that went beyond providing services; it was a testament to our unwavering commitment to creating a haven for dogs, a place where they could experience the highest levels of care, comfort, and companionship. This expansion was not just about accommodating dogs when their owners were away; it was about offering an unmatched lifestyle for our four-legged friends.

Our vision for the luxury dog boarding facility was rooted in a deep understanding of what dogs truly need. We envisioned spacious, comfortable rooms designed to make them feel at home, extensive play areas where they could engage in stimulating activities, and a dedicated team of passionate caregivers who would ensure that every dog felt loved, cherished, and safe during their stay. The facility was more than just a place; it was a sanctuary for our furry guests, embodying our core values of exceptional care and an unwavering commitment to their well-being.

This step in our journey was a testament to our ongoing dedication to canine care. We had already established a strong community of pet experts and launched an innovative dog walking app that aimed to revolutionize the way dogs and their owners experienced care. Now, with the introduction of a physical facility, we are taking the next step in our mission to redefine the standard of care for dogs.

The journey to establish this luxury dog boarding facility was not without its challenges. We needed to ensure that every aspect of the facility met the highest standards of safety, cleanliness, and comfort. This involved meticulous planning, extensive research, and a deep understanding of the needs and preferences of our canine guests.

The Change[20]

As we embarked on this multifaceted journey, the chapters of my entrepreneurial story continued to unfold. It was a journey marked by the power of passion, innovation, and community-building in the ever-expanding world of canine care. With FurBabyLady K-9 Care, we were positioned to lead the way, setting new standards and making a profound impact on the canine industry, one paw at a time.

In reflecting on my entrepreneurial journey, there are three vital lessons that have been instrumental in shaping the success of FurBabyLady K-9 Care: the power of delegation, the magic of collaboration, and the guidance of mentorship.

First and foremost, I learned that delegation is not a sign of weakness but a source of strength. In my initial years as a solo entrepreneur, I had a relentless pursuit of self-reliance. I believed that I needed to personally handle every aspect of the business, from strategy to execution. However, it was only when I learned to entrust tasks to capable hands that I truly began to thrive.

Delegation was a transformative shift that liberated me from the constraints of micromanagement. It allowed me to focus on what I do best, which is nurturing my passion and vision for the brand. It unlocked a world of possibilities and catapulted FurBabyLady K-9 Care to new heights, allowing me to oversee the expansion into luxury dog boarding and the development of the global dog walking app. It was a realization that I couldn't do it all alone and that a team of dedicated and skilled individuals was essential for the brand's growth.

Collaboration was another pivotal aspect of our journey. The magic of working together with like-minded individuals who shared our passion for canines was instrumental in our growth. Through collaboration, we harnessed the collective wisdom and skills of our community of pet experts, each of whom brought a unique perspective to the table.

The power of collaboration extended beyond the internal team. We also built partnerships with other businesses and organizations that shared our values and commitment to canine well-being. These collaborations allowed us to expand our reach, share knowledge, and provide even better services to our clients and their dogs. It was through these collaborations that we were able to set new benchmarks in the canine industry.

Lastly, mentorship played a crucial role in our journey. Having experienced individuals who could offer guidance and support was invaluable. We sought out mentors who had made their mark in the world of entrepreneurship and canine care. Their insights and advice were instrumental in helping us navigate the complexities of the industry and make informed decisions.

In conclusion, the establishment of our luxury dog boarding facility marked a significant chapter in our entrepreneurial journey. It was a testament to our commitment to offering an unparalleled lifestyle for dogs and providing them with a home away from home. The journey was marked by the power of passion, innovation, and community-building, with the expansion into the luxury dog boarding facility serving as a natural progression in our mission to redefine the standard of care for dogs. The lessons we learned along the way – the power of delegation, the magic of collaboration, and the guidance of mentorship – were instrumental in our success and will continue to guide our path as we strive to provide the best in canine care.

As we explore the remarkable journey of FurBabyLady K-9 Care and the passion-driven entrepreneurship in the canine industry, it's evident that following one's heart and unwaveringly pursuing your true passion can lead to incredible achievements. We've witnessed the power of delegation, the magic of collaboration, and the guidance of mentorship, which have been pivotal in shaping our success.

Now, it's your turn to embark on your entrepreneurial journey in the canine world. To help you get started on the right foot, I'm excited to offer you a valuable free gift – the FurBabyLady K-9 Care Checklist. This comprehensive checklist is a reflection of the very essence of what we do. It's a powerful tool for anyone who shares our passion for canine care.

The K-9 Care Checklist serves as a roadmap to excellence, carefully curated with care and expertise. It encapsulates the essential elements that have led to our success and can be instrumental in shaping your journey in the world of canine entrepreneurship. It's a guiding companion that can help you make informed decisions, build meaningful collaborations, and provide top-tier care for our four-legged friends.

Don't hesitate. Take the first step towards your entrepreneurial dreams in the canine industry and let the K-9 Care Checklist be your invaluable guide on this rewarding path. It's time to follow your passion, redefine industry standards, and make a profound impact on the lives of dogs and their owners worldwide. Download your free gift today and start your journey towards canine care excellence.

***

To contact Shantae:

https://10000cards.com/card/iamnaturalblessin

Get Your **Free** Canine Gift: https://k9checklist.com/

You can also follow her on social media:

Facebook: https://www.facebook.com/iamnaturalblessin

Instagram: https://www.instagram.com/furbabyladyk9care/

LinkedIn: https://www.linkedin.com/in/furbabylady/

Shelly Snitko

Shelly Snitko is an independent certified Optavia health coach, business leader, 2-time international best-selling author, speaker, and founder of Caring For Me Too, a faith-based health and wellness community.

She's been married to her college sweetheart, Chris Snitko, for over 40 years. They have two adult children, a son-in-love, four grandsons, and a granddaughter. Together, they've created a life they love in Alabama.

As a business owner, wife, mom, nana, caregiver, friend, and mentor, she understands women's many roles and daily demands. As a 28-year veteran as a caregiver of their adult son with physical disabilities, she has learned to navigate challenging life circumstances, loss, disappointment, and ever-changing responsibilities. She knows what it's like to be

overwhelmed and exhausted caring for others' needs while neglecting her own.

Therefore, Shelly understands that 'caring for me too' isn't selfish; it's a necessity. Self-care doesn't put 'me first,' but prioritizes 'me too,' better equipped to care for loved ones as well as manage the stress and inevitable disappointments that caregivers encounter. It's her passion to empower women (and men) to live their best lives amid life's uncertainties and challenges. Caring For Me Too was birthed from her personal experience of moving from surviving to thriving and reclaiming her identity. With authenticity and vulnerability, she uplifts, inspires, encourages, and supports others toward whole health so they, too, can flourish.

Rising Above the Storm: Embracing Change with Courage

By Shelly Snitko

Storms! Whether caused by nature or life's challenges, they are inevitable. They're as certain as the rising and setting of the sun. One moment, you're going through your day peacefully enjoying the scenery; the next, you're blindsided, caught off-guard by an unexpected storm. Our natural response is to survive.

It's true! Throughout human history, our survival has depended on our ability to navigate and overcome various challenges and threats. Our brains are hardwired to prioritize survival and seek out comfort as a means of ensuring our well-being. That's why when an unexpected storm catches us by surprise, we instinctively elicit a fight-or-flight response.

Have you ever been caught in a storm that crashed in your life, leaving you paralyzed by fear and struggling to stay afloat?

Did you feel overwhelmed, unable to think rationally, reacting out of desperation to survive?

Panic and fear may set off a counterintuitive chain reaction in moments like those. Sometimes, fighting against the storm's turbulence, desperately trying to overpower it and break free, is the exact opposite response needed for survival.

This happened to me several years ago when my husband and I snorkeled off Hanakapiai Beach's coast in Hawaii. We were basking in the beauty of the underwater world, surrounded by a vast array of colorful fish and coral. It was one of those peaceful, surreal moments dreams are made of, with the sun on our backs and the ocean's serenity around us. The moment came to an abrupt halt when I looked up to reorient myself to the shoreline. A rip current had carried us out into the deep unknown ocean waters! Apparently, this area is known for them, but we hadn't received the memo.

Fortunately, as a strong swimmer and a trained lifeguard, I knew what to do. The problem was I panicked; my natural instincts took over. All training forgotten; I started swimming as hard as possible toward the shore—against the current!

Fear overshadowed rational thinking. My husband, seeing me panic, brought me back to my senses. He saw me freaking out until I spotted a rocky ridge nearby. He knew I intended to swim toward it. He, of course, recognized the jagged rocks combined with the intense waves posed a greater danger. Urgently, he tapped my shoulder. I ignored him in my stubbornness, consumed with a resolve to get out of the water as quickly as possible! Unapologetically, he got up in my face and insisted I calm down, listen, and follow him. Reluctantly, I conceded and followed him away from the rocks, parallel to the shoreline, and safely out of danger.

Storms, like rip currents, interrupt our otherwise normal lives, creating chaos and fear, testing our resolve. These storms may vary in nature and intensity, but the choices we make in response to them determine their impact on our lives.

I learned this from personal experience amid a life-altering storm that rocked our world. Eventually, I found myself stuck living in a reactive 'fight-or-flight' state, descending into a pit of despair. I clung to an unhealthy coping mechanism as a lifeline. They provided temporary relief and distraction, but gradually became destructive, posing even greater danger to my health and well-being than the storm itself.

My son's sudden neuromuscular 'storm' became a crucible for learning to face adversity with resilience and adaptability. I hope my story inspires you to navigate your life storms with courage, empowered to move from surviving to thriving.

It was two days after Christmas in 1995, a date etched in my memory as the day life changed forever. In the blink of an eye, our once-bubbly eight-1/2-year-old boy, always brimming with smiles, chatter, and mischief, faced an inexplicable transformation. It was as if a switch had been flipped within his body, seizing control, and robbing him of his ability to perform even the most ordinary tasks—walking, talking, and using his hands. After weeks of numerous procedures and tests, doctors finally diagnosed his condition as a rare neurological movement disorder.

As parents, we felt gut-punched. Stunned, our minds became a whirlwind of emotions, each crashing relentlessly into our consciousness. We had more questions than answers. What did this diagnosis mean? Would this new reality define our son's life? How on earth were we going to deal with this? Uncertainty cast a dark shadow over our hopes and dreams like a heavy fog. The confusion surrounding the diagnosis of 'generalized dystonia' merely compounded our fears.

Life seemed to split into a 'before' and a 'now what' as our family began the strenuous journey of writing the next chapter in our story. In these uncharted waters of life-altering change, where the familiar had transformed into the unknown, we were propelled forward by love, resilience, and an unwavering resolve to conquer whatever obstacles lay in our path.

After six long weeks in the hospital, we returned home. The look of bewilderment in our 6-year-old daughter's eyes mirrored our feelings, as our son had become a different version of himself. He was now confined to a wheelchair, his body plagued by uncontrollable torsion movements that left him unable to walk, talk, or interact as he had just weeks earlier. I wore a brave smile that concealed the overwhelming emotions churning within me.

Determination to overcome obstacles has always been my constant companion. Still, if I'm completely honest, I had no idea where to begin, much less what to expect or the obstacles to conquer. I became driven by the intensity and grit of a storm chaser. With a degree in occupational therapy, a natural inclination to be a control freak, and a mama-bear instinct, I went into 'fix it' mode. My mission was to understand and control this storm called 'generalized dystonia.'

Days turned into months, each marked by a relentless routine of therapies, appointments, and tending to our son's needs—needs that were more demanding than anyone could comprehend. As a wife, mother, and career woman, I already wore many hats. The role of caregiver for our special-needs son added another layer of responsibility to my already busy life. My world spiraled into a never-ending cycle of caregiving, where I constantly put my needs on hold in the name of love and duty.

Years passed in a blur. Amid the stress and constant demands of caregiving, I found myself gradually shrinking while the needs of my family and our son grew. The once driven and vibrant woman in me slowly faded, replaced by a weary caregiver who had forgotten how to care for herself. I had become adept at juggling my son's needs, therapies, and doctor's appointments, yet I couldn't even remember the last time I pursued a hobby or took a moment to breathe. I mourned the loss of my career and my ministry to women.

As the years continued, my son graduated high school, and his care demanded increased time and physical strength. I no longer had the freedom or energy to come and go as I once had. While others saw a strong woman who seemingly navigated life's challenges with ease, beneath the surface, my constant companions were discouragement and defeat. As friends stopped calling and relationships eroded, feelings of bitterness, isolation, loneliness, and depression flourished.

My identity had become so immersed in caregiving that I lost myself. I found I was increasingly dissatisfied with life even though, apart from the challenges of caregiving, I had a good life. I felt trapped in a life I never expected. Questions flooded my mind. "How did I get here? What happened to the woman I used to be? Is change possible? Will I ever get unstuck and find my way back to me?" I didn't have answers. The only thing I knew was I couldn't live this way anymore!

Can anyone relate?

Have you ever felt trapped, lost in a dark pit of despair, unable to find your way out?

Twenty-two years I lived stuck, simply surviving! The chronic stress and fear associated with my son's dystonia held me captive. The crutches I used for comfort, escape, and security no longer served me. Six years ago, something changed. I was suddenly awakened from 'sleepwalking' through my life. It marked a turning point for me!

The Change[20]

My wake-up call came when my daughter shared family pictures of our grandsons enjoying an Easter egg hunt in our backyard. What I saw in those photos shocked me. The boys were having a blast, energetic and all smiles. However, in stark contrast was me, a woman I barely recognized—she seemed to carry the weight of the world on her shoulders. She looked miserable, overweight, exhausted, and overcome by life.

A wave of realization coursed through me like a bolt of lightning. "I'm sick and tired of being sick and tired!" The devotion that had driven me to care for our son had come at a high cost—the cost of losing myself. As I looked at my reflection, I knew I needed to make some changes. It was glaringly apparent that what I'd been doing wasn't working. Though it was painful to see the person I'd become, it proved to be the catalyst igniting a fire within me—I was determined to reclaim my identity and find a balance between being a loving caregiver and nurturing my mind, body, and soul.

"*If nothing changes, nothing changes. If you keep doing what you're doing, you're going to keep getting what you're getting. If you want change, make some,*" this quote by Courtney C. Stevens became my mantra.

One of my biggest challenges was finding time for myself and maintaining a healthy lifestyle amid the daily caregiving responsibilities. For as long as I could remember, I had been fighting against the 'current,' trying to fix my son's dystonia. The harder I fought; the worse things got. I finally accepted this hard truth: my circumstances were not keeping me stuck, it was the choices I'd made in response to them! To get unstuck meant taking my power back, choosing to change, and reclaim my life.

No doubt, making meaningful changes is tough. It all starts with our thoughts. Our willingness to let go of the obstacles is crucial. Change isn't just about doing things differently; it's about changing how we think, which paves the way for new possibilities. This shift in perspective is the spark that drives us toward positive change.

Socrates once wisely said, 'The secret of change is to focus all of your energy not on fighting the old, but on building the new.' It's essential to draw lessons from our past experiences without becoming consumed by them. I realized that my approach to dealing with my son's dystonia was rooted in a desperate need for survival. I immersed myself in research, scouring the internet for any potential treatment or information that could cure or better manage his condition. When these treatments fell short, seeds of bitterness took root. Food, particularly unhealthy options, became a source of comfort, numbing the frustration and disappointment I couldn't process. Excessive busyness became my escape from a life that seemed beyond control.

Over time, these coping mechanisms had turned into significant obstacles. Instead of providing comfort, they had become shackles that held me captive. As years passed, they transformed into unhealthy habits and addictive behaviors, hiding deeper issues beneath the surface.

For years, I had been expending my energy in a fruitless battle, attempting to change aspects of life beyond my control. It gradually became evident that I needed to redirect my focus and attention toward nurturing the change within myself.

Have you ever yearned to flourish in life but discovered that you were pushing back against change?

What comforts have you clung to, even when they no longer propel you forward?

It wasn't until I acknowledged the detrimental effects of my unhealthy coping strategies that I quit using them as excuses. It demanded courage to release my old habits, overcome the obstacles, and wholeheartedly embrace my fear of change. It was the first step towards taking charge of my life.

Courage empowered me to leave behind old habits, routines, and beliefs in exchange for new opportunities and possibilities. It allowed me to acknowledge my fears, confront them, and move forward, not despite them but because of them. This newfound courage was the driving force behind my decision to address my weight gain, a consequence of years of unhealthy eating habits. In my pursuit of transformation, I conducted extensive research and stumbled upon a comprehensive program that offered the tools, strategies, and skills I needed to create a healthier version of myself.

My heart resonated with the mission of Optavia: 'Lifelong Transformation, One Healthy Habit At A Time TM.' This four-component program provided a structured framework to guide me along the way. It included a health coach for accountability and support, a vibrant community that understood the unique challenges I faced as a special needs mom, a Habits of Health Transformational System to reshape my mindset for necessary behavioral and lifestyle modifications, and a simple, straightforward nutrition plan promising predictable results for my success.

Losing 50 pounds in just over four months was a remarkable achievement, but it represented more than just an external transformation. This journey became the catalyst for profound personal growth beyond my wildest dreams. It unveiled the unhealthy roles I had adopted as coping mechanisms for life's challenges. I often oscillated between playing the hero, trying to save the day, and assuming the victim role, searching for someone or something to blame. Psychologist Stephen Karpman describes this as living in the Drama Triangle, where individuals adopt dysfunctional roles when confronted with painful circumstances beyond their control. When life doesn't unfold as expected, we tend to look for someone or something to hold responsible.

My internal dialogue often wavered between two extremes: 'Poor, poor pitiful me!' and 'Look out, help is on the way, dear, help is on the way.' When I played the victim, I felt like life had dealt me an unfair hand, leaving me helpless and incapable of finding joy. On the other hand, when I assumed the hero role, I became obsessed with fixing and controlling everything, neglecting my anxiety, emotions, and deeper issues. This constant cycle of unrest, anxiety, and chronic stress had woven itself into the fabric of my life, leading to the development of unhealthy habits and thought patterns. I had unintentionally trapped myself in what psychologists call the 'drama triangle' by neglecting self-care and undervaluing my physical, emotional, mental, and spiritual well-being.

Have you ever felt like you were stuck in your own life's drama?

Perhaps, like me, you wished for change but found yourself caught up in negative thoughts and feelings of failure. It's a common struggle – wanting things to be different but feeling held back by the habits and ways of dealing with life that we're used to.

As I started on the journey of making changes, I discovered that resilience could grow within me. However, I learned that these seeds of resilience need the right conditions to thrive. Until now, my old habits and ways of thinking have acted like roadblocks to change. I had relied on emotional eating, busyness, and relentlessly trying to 'fix' my son's dystonia as ways to protect myself from life's challenges. As Brene Brown points out, 'When you try to ignore and push away disappointment and tough emotions, you unintentionally push down all emotions, including joy.' My choices had unintentionally led me to live in constant disappointment. But now, as I work on my personal growth, I've come to realize that building resilience means facing uncomfortable emotions head-on and embracing the full range of human experiences.

As a woman of faith, I rediscovered my joy in living when I let go of bitterness and resentment towards God. Through the trials and lessons that life has brought my way, I've discovered a deeper sense of purpose that fills me with passion. It drives me to stand alongside other caregivers and special needs moms who carry the weight of constant responsibilities and demands on their time and energy. As a health coach, guiding others through the same program that transformed my life, my mission has become clear: to empower others to regain control of their lives. I offer not only solutions for weight management but also the promise of more energy, increased confidence, financial stability, and the importance of self-care."

'Caring For Me Too' has emerged from my own experiences, and my vision is to ignite a global movement that revolutionizes the caregiving experience by fostering a culture of self-care and resilience. I envision a world where women, caregivers, and special needs moms feel supported, empowered, and equipped to prioritize their well-being. This, in turn, empowers them to provide the best possible care for their loved ones without compromising their health and happiness.

As you reflect on your life, consider the crucial lessons from the current story: life's disruptions can serve as catalysts for positive change. Courage is required to confront the unpredictable twists and turns they produce. But you possess the power to rise above adversity with purpose and resilience. It's your choice! I firmly believe your storm is an opportunity for you not just to survive but to thrive – **not despite the challenges but because of them!**

"When it seems as though you are facing nothing but difficulties, see it as an invaluable opportunity to experience the greatest joy that you can! For you know that when your faith is tested it stirs up in you the power of endurance. And then as your endurance grows even stronger, it will release perfection into every part of your being until there is nothing missing and nothing lacking." James 1:2-4 TPT

***

To contact Shelly:

https://caringformetoo.com or https://linktr.ee/slsnitkocaringformetoo

Facebook https://www.facebook.com/shelly.snitko

Instagram https://www.instagram.com/shellysnitko_caringformetoo/

Samantha Duffy

Samantha Duffy is a highly gifted and talented woman who is passionate about sharing with others what she has learned over a lifetime of research and application of principles and techniques that helps one get in touch with true energy source that feeds their personal development. In addition, she has a wealth of knowledge and personal experience that encompassed everything from business, academia, parenting, relationships, energy, spirituality, and a vast amount of life experiences through significant extreme radical personal and professional changes. She has spent a significant amount of time, research, and money on her own personal self-development that brings her to become the best version of herself everyday. Her mentoring and motivational skills are exceptional, whilst her kind, considerate, and intelligent approach naturally creates a comfortable dynamic in all her relationships.

A Simple Idea

By Samantha Duffy

I believe I understand how a thought is created. This knowledge has fundamentally changed the way I perceive everything. It has illuminated a belief in me that makes everything possible. After this knowledge came to me, I have accumulated such a tremendous amount of additional knowledge and understanding on how everything that ever were to exist works. I tapped into a power that is so incredible strong. This power helps to shape our lives in the way we understand ourselves, our lives, our creations, and the universe today. Once we tap into the power of our innate intelligence, we have the ability to change the direction of our life.

A thought is an answer to a question or the question itself. It's as simple as that. We elaborate on these answers to better justify our rationale for the answer we are delivering. I believe that the very first thoughts we have upon birth are the who, what, where, when and why questions. Then our subconscious mind takes action and immediately starts seeking its answer. There isn't a single question we can ask that we don't already have the answer to. I know this because I have discovered that every answer is based on the fundamental innate intelligence that we are all born with. Every person that ever has existed on earth, or perhaps beyond, has the same core functional knowledge. We are born with a system operating manual that has the explicit instructions as to how every aspect of the human body, mind, energy, light, and soul operate. We know everything right from the very second we take our first breath of air and our consciousness awakens ready to understand where we just arrived.

Luckily for us, we are created so perfectly that we don't need to understand the details of everything little thing right up front. As we encounter new information, we open ourselves up to more opportunities to explore and remember the knowledge we already have. However, that doesn't mean we don't know the answer. The initial questions of who, what where, when and why that we ask is asked to our subconscious mind. Then the job of the subconscious mind is two part. First, it seeks an answer to every question asked and doesn't give up until it comes to the conclusion that either the question was not a logical one or provides an answer that makes sense based on the knowledge it has at the time. Second, it operates in a continuous improvement mindset where it evaluates the information known and the new incoming information to find the best balance of the two and update and course correct prior knowledge and beliefs. Every time a question is asked the subconscious mind evaluates all of its existing knowledge and then looks for possible synergies of that knowledge to determine the proper answer or solution to the question.

What I find most interesting is the original source of knowledge it starts with. The way the human body, mind, energy, light, and soul operate is absolutely the most magnificently interesting information in all of time and space. We are so precisely constructed. It is completely mind blowing the intricacies of the way we operate. All of that knowledge is what we are born with. It is innate intelligence. What is completely fascinating to me though is that I discovered that everything we have ever created in all of our existences across all lifetimes is based on that very innate intelligence. There is nothing that we have created or that we do as a profession that isn't tied back to this fundamental knowledge that we are born with. So, what that means is that every single person to every exist has had the opportunity to have created anything that currently or will exist, as well work in any profession. However, that requires some substantial amount of realignment between the mind, body and emotion. It is imperative that one seeks to understand its core belief system and connect via spiritual growth to the subconscious mind. It is not a very simple thing to do as it requires a substantial amount of self-reflection.

The knowledge that we are born with includes all the basics of how we operate. These operations of the human body can be directly reflected in the things that we have created and what we do for our professions. The fundamental knowledge of how electricity works was based on our own knowledge of our the brain and the energy of the body have synchronized. The way our body processes our food can be directly reflected in how we have set up our plumbing systems, crafted our vitamins packages, and filter and dispose of waste. The way cameras, videos, microphones, and speakers work correspond accordingly to way that our brain interacts with our eyes, memory, hearing, and voice box. This has also been duplicated in the way that the data our brain receives, filters, and regurgitates data via our WIFI set up and televisions. The simplest example is the brain itself. We created a computer which duplicates the same basic concept that our brain by processing information, creating content, and running core operations behind the scenes with little to no impact on the day-to-day operations. Even the basic concept of putting things in motion is based on our body being in motion. We have utensils via our hands and nails, and a garbage disposal in our mouth. Our body hair clothed us perfectly fine for a significant portion of our existence. Our housing insulation can be represented via the fat layering of our body, as well as setting up the foundational structure via our skeleton. Our energy is so powerful that it helps us regulate our internal thermostats. We also have used the basic concept of burning things to cleanse, just like fevers burn off bacteria and viruses we catch. We like to decorate our bodies, just the same way we decorate walls and our environment. We filter the air in both our lungs and our air conditioning units. Our vehicles motor system mirrors to a degree the way our heart regulates our body. This is an endless list. If you look around the world, you will see that everything we have ever created can be tied directly back to the operations manual of the human along with synergies with other known previous creations.

We can tie every profession back to either educate, maintain, grow, entertain or protect the self. We have teachers, leaders, mentors, coaches, parents, and trainers to educate us on the wonders of the universe and ourselves. We have doctors, psychologists, nutritionists, dentists, fitness trainers, chefs, and government officials to maintain our lives and existence. We have all the different companies with their unique services and products in the business world to help us create more, grow and entertain us. We have military, police, and firefighters to protect us. We even have chemists that have been able to determine exactly the perfect balance of chemicals to help get the body back to its expected levels after it is exposed to bodily or mental traumas. The knowledge they all have to do their jobs properly is based on knowledge that we have to operate ourselves. This all ties back directly to each question that we ask ourselves and then patiently wait for the subconscious mind to find the perfect solution. That is how we educated ourselves to be able to do each profession that currently is in place.

Our emotions are the single driver of how each person becomes a unique individual to some degree. The way we emotionally respond to the environmental stimuli creates unique experiences that drive us to become more or less interested in specific areas of life and existence. That is the part that can also block people from becoming the best and most creative self. That is why understanding where these blocks lay is a critical component to aligning with the mind, body and emotion. Once you work with a coach to help identify your personal limiting beliefs and restructure your thought process appropriately you will then have an opportunity to truly change your life. Absorbing the information just presented helps you understand that everyone is created completely equally and has an opportunity to successfully do or create anything they want.

***

To contact Samantha:

www.innateintelligence.biz

Samantha@innateintelligence.biz

(805) 422-4795

Fanny Newport

Fanny Newport has a bachelor's degree in Management and Business Administration and speaks 3 languages fluently.

After surviving the 1994 genocide in Rwanda and losing many loved ones, including her father, she came to Canada as a refugee, didn't speak English but she worked hard and:

- built a 7 figure Real Estate portfolio from scratch,
- Co-authored a Best-Selling book with **Brian Tracy**
- Was featured on some local Radio and podcasts
- Shared the stage with legends like:

    Robert Kiyosaki, author of Rich Dad, Poor Dad,

    Robert G. Allen, author of No Money Down,

    Kevin Harrington from the TV show Shark Tank,

    Michele Romanow from the TV show Dragons' Den, and many others.

Fanny used what happened to her, to become resilient, and focus on the positive, and now she teaches others how to stay positive when life gets tough.

She is a lifelong learner; she keeps improving her skills and knowledge.

Resilience and Positive Mindset Are Key for Any Business

By Fanny Newport, BBA

Let's face it, life is full of surprises, both good and not-so-good ones. But in business, there are even more struggles, especially at the beginning. There are hard times and countless problems before success. That's why you need to have resilience and a positive mindset to survive and thrive.

Resilience

> *"When fear rushed in, I learned how to hear my heart racing but refused to allow my feelings to sway me".*
>
> *— Coretta Scott King*

What Does Resilience Mean?

Resilience means knowing how to cope despite setbacks, barriers, or limited resources. Resilience is a measure of how much you want something and how much you are willing and able to overcome obstacles to get it. It has to do with your emotional strength. It's the capacity to recover quickly from difficulties, and toughness.

When we come across a problem, the choices we make determine how resilient we can be.

For example, if you are at the traffic light and someone hits your car because they didn't stop. How do you react? Do you get mad and yell and make a big scene? Or do you stay calm and talk to them and not let that incident destroy the rest of your day? How about when you don't get the promotion you were expecting? Do you get mad and blame everybody and be mad the whole day? Or do you try to understand why you didn't get it and see what you can correct to get it when the next opportunity comes?

No matter what happens in our lives, we always have two choices: we can either face the problem and try to find the solution or we can choose to let fear control us and make excuses.

Face your fears and doubts, and new worlds will open to you.

— *Robert Kiyosaki*

How Being Humble Can Help in Developing Resilience?

Growing up, my parents used to tell us that we have to be humble all the time, especially when everything is really good, we had to be happy but be careful not let that moment control us, because things can change quickly.

You can be successful today and lose everything tomorrow. They used to tell us that if you make fun of someone because you are better than them, the situation may change and they or someone else will be better than you and they won't forget how you treated them. That taught me to control my emotions and to develop resilience.

Being humble can significantly contribute to the development of resilience by fostering a mindset and approach to life that is conducive to bouncing back from challenges. Talking about challenges, when I was at university in Rwanda, we experienced power outages every evening when I needed to study.

As electricity was restored around midnight when everyone was asleep, I opted to go to bed right after school, around 6:30 pm, wake up at 2 am, and study until the morning when it was time to return to school. It was challenging; I didn't like to wake up while everyone else was sleeping, and the nights were cold, but I knew that to succeed I had to do it. I couldn't wait for the time when I would go to bed when I wanted and sleep in whenever I wanted. It seemed like a luxury to me. It was difficult, coming from school and going to bed right away while everybody else was still awake, watching TV, and spending time together, but I had to make that choice. I didn't like it but the satisfaction on the day of my graduation far surpassed that and the sleepless nights I endured to get there.

"*What you get by achieving your goals is not as important as what you become by achieving your goals*".

— *Zig Ziglar*

That keeps reminding me that if I want something, it doesn't matter how ugly or uncomfortable my present situation can be, I have to focus on the result and keep going until I get to where I want to be. Trust me, when you get there, you will be so happy that the struggle you went through becomes insignificant. The satisfaction, happiness, and joy you will experience are greater than the hardship you went through to get there.

In every hard situation, we have 2 choices of pain: the pain of discipline or the pain of regret and disappointment, choose wisely.

You Solve One Problem and Then Another One Comes Up.

When I moved to London, Ontario, I had to take the test to obtain my Ontario driver's license, as the one I had wasn't recognized, and I failed the exam three times before succeeding. The mistake I made was that every time I failed, I would go back and attempt it again without first acknowledging why I failed.

It felt as if I kept bumping against the wall, hoping this wall would open. But before banging against the wall, check first if the wall is made of concrete, bricks, or cardboard. If the wall is brick or concrete, the solution is not to break it but to see how to get around it or climb it.

> *Insanity is doing the same thing over and over again, and expecting different results"*
>
> *– Albert Einstein.*

After failing for the 3rd time, that's when I realized that I could keep doing it a hundred times, and I would keep getting the same result. I stopped blaming others and learned from my mistakes and finally I got my driver's license. Many times, when things don't go as we planned, we like to blame others instead of facing the problem, analyzing what happened, and correcting the mistakes.

> *"Obstacles don't have to stop you. If you run into a wall, don't turn around and give up. Figure out how to climb it, go through it, or work around it."*
>
> *— Michael Jordan*

When you start or run a business, you'll come across many problems, maybe you don't have enough customers, maybe people don't know your product or service yet, maybe your employees or associates are stealing from you....

But you still have to pay your bills, you still have to pay your employees or your rent. That's why you need to develop resilience.

"When something is important enough, you do it even if the odds are not in your favor".

— Elon Musk

How Can You Develop Resilience?

Developing resilience is a gradual process that involves adopting certain practices and perspectives. You can develop resilience by:

Cultivating a Positive Mindset: Focus on positive aspects of situations or reframe challenges as opportunities for growth.

Developing Problem-Solving Skills: Break down problems into smaller and manageable parts and identify concrete steps to address each part of the problem.

Set Realistic, achievable, and meaningful goals.

Celebrate small victories along the way, don't wait until you reach the big goal, celebrate even the small achievements, it will motivate you to keep going.

Be honest: When you make a mistake, examine what happened and find a solution. Avoid blaming others. Not accepting your mistakes and shifting blame leads to repeating the same errors. Remember, when you point a finger at others, three fingers point back at you.

Don't let emotions control you, when times are tough, stay calm, remind yourself that everything happens for a reason, and try to find the reason behind what happened or the lessons you learn from it.

Focus on the result you want and don't let the problem distract you from it.

Remember, you solve one problem, and another one comes up, stay strong and keep going, and always stay focused and prepared for the next challenge.

It doesn't matter how many times you fail, what matters is that you pick yourself up and try again, losing is part of the process to success, so keep hustling.

"I've missed more than 9000 shots in my career. I've lost almost 300 games.

26 times. I've been trusted to take the game winning shot and missed.

I've failed over and over and over again in my life. And that is why I succeed. "

— Michael Jordan

Remember, developing resilience is a continuous process, and different strategies work for different people. It involves building a set of skills and attitudes that help you navigate life's challenges with strength and adaptability.

In business and life, we need to be resilient so we can keep moving forward.

Positive Mindset

"Positive thinking will let you do everything better than negative thinking will".

— Zig Ziglar

As we just said, life is sometimes hard, and to be able to develop resilience, we need a positive mindset. When we think positively or we experience positive emotions, we give ourselves the power to deal with any problem, and therefore, challenges are considered temporary and can be overcome.

On the other hand, when we are having negative thoughts, we cannot think properly which makes it difficult to navigate challenging situations and may lead to a bad decision.

Nobody likes to spend time with negative people, who criticize others, complain all the time, or don't appreciate anything. People like to spend time with positive and happy people. Did you know that our brain is constantly monitoring the emotional tone of our thoughts?

When you are having many negative thoughts, your brain responds by creating stress and sadness in your body. When you add more positive thoughts, your brain will create relaxation and happiness, and you will feel happy. We need to create a positive environment and get rid of any negative thoughts, we also need to stay away from negative people, they drain our energy, they find problems for everything.

Many times, your loved ones are the ones who don't support or believe in you, and that hurts. But you have to remember why you started already or why you want to start. It's your goal, not theirs.

Remember that people judge you from their perspective, they will try to tell you how to run your business even though they never run or own any business. Their advice is to play it safe and stay where you are, instead of taking the risk of starting a business. To be able to face that every day, you need to have a positive mindset. It's your life, not somebody else's, you have to do whatever it takes to succeed. You are responsible for your failure and your success.

> *"Never give up. Today is hard, tomorrow will be worse. But the day after tomorrow will be sunshine"*
>
> — Jack Ma

I remember living in a small apartment in Montreal looking for a job. I didn't have money but I had hope that soon I would have enough money to do what I wanted. Even though I was afraid that I wouldn't have enough money to pay rent or buy food, I stayed positive. I didn't let fear stop me, in my mind, that was just a temporary challenge. To encourage myself, I went to the Dollar store and bought a keychain with the $100 bill on it. Every single day I would look at my hundred-dollar keychain and tell myself that very soon I will have many $100 bills. I kept thinking positively and I got 3 jobs: the first one was during the day, Monday to Friday, the second in the evenings, and the third one on weekends. No need to say that, that time, the $100 were real bills.

We attract what we focus on, so focus on what you want.

How Can You Develop a Positive Mindset?

Start your day with a positive attitude, when you wake up, tell yourself that today is a good day, you are going to accomplish a lot and you are happy. The way you start your morning can determine the rest of your day, stay away from the news, and start your day with positive affirmations, good music, or whatever makes you happy.

Turn your negative self-talk into a positive one. Instead of saying, 'I'm so stupid,' consider saying, 'That was a mistake. How can I correct it? What went wrong?' Rather than thinking 'I'm not good,' shift to 'I need to practice this. I will improve.

Appreciate small wins. When you don't finish what you planned, acknowledge that you accomplished something—perhaps you finished half. Be happy about that progress, and plan to complete the rest as soon as possible. Don't wait for everything to be perfect; celebrate every step.

Every day, appreciate small things. Like being able to breathe when some people have to buy oxygen at the hospital. Appreciate the sun, the rain, the flowers, and more.

When you fail, don't fail to learn: When you make a mistake, don't be too hard on yourself, learn from your mistakes. Better yet, learn from other people's mistakes as much as you can.

Turn bad situations into opportunities. For instance, if your appointment gets canceled at the last minute, rather than getting upset, utilize that time for something meaningful or essential to you. Be flexible; you could send that message you hadn't had a chance to send yet or make a call you wanted to make.

A few years ago, my previous employer informed me that I no longer had a job after 14 years of working there. Instead of panicking, I saw it as an opportunity for something better. I told myself, that means I'm going to get a better job. Surprisingly it worked: the same day I left another employer called me to offer me a job. I'm grateful that when it occurred, I had already developed a positive mindset, otherwise it was going to be hard and stressful.

Sometimes, life can be very hard, but we have to keep moving. I believe that every single person has a purpose on this earth, I believe that we all have to serve each other somehow. If you start a business, you will be helping your employees and your customers, you will be touching many lives directly and indirectly. Even a smile can change somebody's day. Stay positive all the time, keep moving forward, celebrate the small wins and you will accomplish a lot.

Our greatest weakness lies in giving up.

The most certain way to succeed is always to try just one more time.

— Thomas A. Edison

***

To contact Fanny:

info@greenmineproperties.com

https://www.instagram.com/greenmineproperties/

https://www.linkedin.com/in/greenmine-properties-113989170/

https://www.facebook.com/greenmine.properties/

https://www.youtube.com/@greenmineproperties9821

Afterword

Life is always a series of transitions… people, places and things that shape who we are as individuals. Often, you never know that the next catalyst for change is around the corner.

Jim Britt and Jim Lutes have spent decades influencing individuals to blossom into the best version of themselves.

Allow all you have read in this book to create introspection and redirection if required. It's your journey to craft.

The Change is a series. A global movement. Watch for future releases and add them to your collection. If you know of anyone who would like to be considered as a co-author for a future book, have them email our offices at support@jimbritt.com.

The individual and combined works of Jim Britt and Jim Lutes have filled seminar rooms to maximum capacity and created a worldwide demand.

The blessings go both ways as Jim and Jim are always willing students of life. Out of demand for life-changing programs and events, Jim and Jim conduct seminars worldwide.

To Schedule Jim Britt or Jim Lutes as your featured speaker at your next convention or special event, email Jim Britt at: support@jimbritt.com or Jim Lutes at: mindpowerpro@yahoo.com

For more info on Jim & Jim visit: www.LutesInternational.com or www.JimBritt.com

For information on Jim Britt's online coaching course Cracking the Rich Code: http://CrackingTheRichCode.com

Master your moment as they become hours that become days.

Do something remarkable today! Your legacy awaits.

Blessings,

Jim Britt and Jim Lutes

www.ingramcontent.com/pod-product-compliance
Lightning Source LLC
LaVergne TN
LVHW010159070526
838199LV00062B/4421